DIABETIC
Candy, Cookie & Dessert
Cookbook

DIABETIC
Candy, Cookie & Dessert
Cookbook

Mary Jane Finsand

 Sterling Publishing Co., Inc.   New York

By the same author
Caring & Cooking for the Hyperactive Child
The Complete Diabetic Cookbook

Library of Congress Cataloging in Publication Data
Finsand, Mary Jane.
    Diabetic candy, cookie & dessert cookbook.

    Includes index.
    1. Diabetes—Diet therapy—Recipes.   2. Confectionery
3. Desserts.   I. Title.
RC662.F563   641.8'6   81-85024
ISBN 0-8069-5568-6   AACR2
ISBN 0-8069-5569-4 (lib. bdg.)
ISBN 0-8069-7586-5 (pbk.)

Copyright © 1982 by Mary Jane Finsand
Published by Sterling Publishing Co., Inc.
Two Park Avenue, New York, N.Y. 10016
Distributed in Australia by Oak Tree Press Co., Ltd.
P.O. Box K514 Haymarket, Sydney 2000, N.S.W.
Distributed in the United Kingdom by Blandford Press
Link House, West Street, Poole, Dorset BH15 1LL, England
Distributed in Canada by Oak Tree Press Ltd.
% Canadian Manda Group, 215 Lakeshore Boulevard East
Toronto, Ontario M5A 3W9
Manufactured in the United States of America

Contents

Foreword

Sucrose is a high energy food that tastes sweet. Humans tend to enjoy dessert sweets and eat more sugar than they should. In addition, diabetics must restrict and control their sucrose intake within a medically planned diet of nutritious meals.

Whether we like it or not, every person is in fact, "on a diet." A diet can be planned, or a diet can be accidental; a diet can be restricted, or a diet can be unlimited. A diet is the actual food that we eat. A *planned* diet is a specific premeditated food *outline* that is designed to supply our bodies with the proper types and proportions of foods for optimum health. Mary Jane Finsand's *Diabetic Candy, Cookie & Dessert Cookbook* is an excellent aid in preparing a wide range of delicious sweets for diabetics, weight dieters, and other persons interested in reducing sucrose intake while practicing good dietary nutritional habits.

Complete calorie and food exchange information is included with each recipe. This allows users to easily regulate food intake within a medical doctor's recommendations. An additional feature includes a choice of either customary (cups, ounces, etc.) or metric (millilitres, grams, etc.) measures.

I believe that this cookbook will be an invaluable aid to individuals and families who like to eat sweet-tasting foods and still follow recommended nutritional habits. Mary Jane has created another excellent medically sound kitchen reference to complement her previous book, *The Complete Diabetic Cookbook*.

JAMES D. HEALY, M.D., F.A.A.P.

Introduction

Here it is, the *Diabetic Candy, Cookie & Dessert Cookbook*. In *The Complete Diabetic Cookbook*, I said I wanted to help remove the word "restricted" from the diabetic diet. I just did not realize there were so many people who had a sweet tooth or did not feel a meal was complete without a dessert.

Eating a piece of pie or candy bar without knowing the exchange value or calorie count can be disastrous to any diet. All of us should be aware of our total calorie intake and compare it to our total calorie output daily. Overweight is a deterrent to good physical health. To make weight reduction or a health diet as pleasant as possible, it is important to realize that eating can still be made an enjoyable experience. In designing any diet, one should allow for a few "fun" foods once in a while. This is possible when we know both the exchange value and the calorie count in those "fun" foods and consider them in our daily calorie or exchange intake.

It would be absurd to say that a dieter can eat dessert after every meal. You cannot, and you know it. But you can allow yourself a little freedom within your diet. Just know what you are eating.

I wish to thank the friends who have given of their time, recipes and taste knowledge in the preparation of this book. I hope you will find that this cookbook will help you with your food selection and keep you on a good balanced diet.

MARY JANE FINSAND

Sugar Replacements and Your Diet

Your diet has been prescribed by a doctor or diet counselor, who has been trained to determine your diet requirements by considering your exercise and daily life patterns. DO NOT try to outguess them. Always stay within the guidelines of your individual diet, and ask your counselor about additions or substitutions in your diet. If you have any questions about any diabetic recipes or exchanges, ask your diet counselor.

Most sweeteners or sugar replacements can be found in your supermarket. They vary in sweetness, aftertaste, aroma and calories. The listing below is by ingredient name rather than product name. Check the side of the box or bottle to determine the contents of the product.

Aspartame and aspartame products are new to the supermarket. Aspartame is a natural protein sweetener. It is not an artificial sweetener, but because of its intense sweetness it reduces calories and carbohydrates in the diet. It has no aftertaste and has a sweet aroma. It does lose part of its sweetness in heating and is recommended for use in cold products.

Cyclamates and products containing cyclamates are less intense as sweeteners than the saccharin products, but also leave a bitter aftertaste. Many of our sugar replacements are a combination of saccharin and cyclamates.

Fructose is commonly known as fruit sugar. It is a naturally occurring sugar found in fruits and honey. The taste of fruit sugar (fructose) is the same as that of common table sugar (sucrose), but because of intense sweetness, it will reduce calories and carbohydrates in the diet. It is not affected by heat or cooling.

Glycyrrhizen and products containing glycyrrhizen are as intense a sweetener as saccharin. They are seen less in supermarkets because they give the food products a licorice taste and aroma.

Saccharin and products containing saccharin are the most widely known and used of the intense sweeteners. When used in baking or cooking, saccharin has a bitter lingering aftertaste. You will normally find it in the form of sodium saccharin in products labelled low-calorie sugar replacements.

Granular or dry sugar replacements containing sodium saccharin give less aftertaste to foods that are heated.

Liquid sugar replacements containing sodium saccharin are best used in cold foods or entered into the food after it has partially cooled and no longer needs any heating.

Sorbitol is used in many of our commercial food products. It has little or no aftertaste and has a sweet aroma. At present it can only be bought in bulk form at health food stores.

Using the Recipes for Your Diet

All recipes have been developed using diet substitutions for sugar, syrup, toppings, puddings, gelatins and imitation or lo-cal dairy and nondairy products.

Read the recipes carefully, then assemble all equipment and ingredients. Use standard measuring equipment (whether metric or customary, be sure to measure accurately). Substitutions or additions of herbs and spices or flavorings to a recipe may be made by using the guide for Spices and Herbs or for Flavorings and Extracts; they will make any of the recipes distinctively your own.

CUSTOMARY TERMS

t.	teaspoon
T.	tablespoon
c.	cup
pkg.	package
pt.	pint
qt.	quart
oz.	ounce
lb.	pound
°F	degrees Fahrenheit
in.	inch

METRIC SYMBOLS

mL	millilitre
L	litre
g	gram
kg	kilogram
°C	degrees Celsius
mm	millimetre
cm	centimetre

Cooking Pans and Casseroles

Customary:	Metric:
1 qt.	1 L
2 qt.	2 L
3 qt.	3 L

OVEN COOKING GUIDES

Fahrenheit °F	Oven Heat	Celsius °C
250–275	very slow	120–135
300–325	slow	150–165
350–375	moderate	177–190
400–425	hot	200–220
450–475	very hot	230–245
475–500	hottest	250–290

Use this candy thermometer guide to test for doneness:

Fahrenheit °F	Test		Celsius °C
230–234	Syrup:	Thread	100–112
234–240	Fondant/Fudge:	Soft Ball	112–115
244–248	Caramels:	Firm Ball	118–120
250–266	Marshmallows:	Hard Ball	121–130
270–290	Taffy:	Soft Crack	132–143
300–310	Brittle:	Hard Crack	149–154

10

GUIDE TO APPROXIMATE EQUIVALENTS

Customary:				Metric:	
ounces; pounds	cups	tablespoons	teaspoons	millilitres	grams; kilograms
			¼ t.	1 mL	1 g
			½ t.	2 mL	
			1 t.	5 mL	
			2 t.	10 mL	
½ oz.		1 T.	3 t.	15 mL	15 g
1 oz.		2 T.	6 t.	30 mL	30 g
2 oz.	¼ c.	4 T.	12 t.	60 mL	
4 oz.	½ c.	8 T.	24 t.	125 mL	
8 oz.	1 c.	16 T.	48 t.	250 mL	
2.2 lb.					1 kg

Keep in mind that this is not an exact conversion, but generally may
be used for food measurement.

GUIDE TO PAN SIZES

Baking Pans

Customary:	Metric:	Holds:	Holds (metric):
8-in. pie	20-cm pie	2 c.	600 mL
9-in. pie	23-cm pie	1 qt.	1 L
10-in. pie	25-cm pie	1¼ qt.	1.3 L
8-in. pie	20-cm round	1 qt.	1 L
9-in. pie	23-cm round	1½ qt.	1.5 L
8-in. square	20-cm square	2 qt.	2 L
9-in. square	23-cm square	2½ qt.	2.5 L
9 × 5 × 2-in. loaf	23 × 13 × 18-cm loaf	2 qt.	2 L
9-in. tube	23-cm tube	3 qt.	3 L
10-in. tube	25-cm tube	3 qt.	3 L
10-in. Bundt^{T}	25-cm Bundt^{T}	1 qt.	1 L
9 × 5 in.	23 × 13 cm	1½ qt.	1.5 L
10 × 6 in.	25 × 16 cm	3½ qt.	3.5 L
13 × 9 × 2 in.	33 × 23 × 5 cm	3½ qt.	3.5 L
14 × 10 in.	36 × 25 cm		cookie tin
15½ × 10½ × 1 in.	39 × 25 × 3 cm		jelly roll

FLAVORINGS AND EXTRACTS

Orange, lime, and lemon peels give vegetables, pastries and puddings a fresh, clean flavor; liquor flavors, such as brandy or rum, give cakes and other desserts a company flare. Choose from the following to add some zip, without adding calories:

Almond	Butter Rum	Pecan
Anise (Licorice)	Cherry	Peppermint
Apricot	Clove	Pineapple
Banana Crème	Coconut	Raspberry
Blackberry	Grape	Rum
Black Walnut	Hazelnut	Sassafras
Blueberry	Lemon	Sherry
Brandy	Lime	Strawberry
Butter	Mint	Vanilla
Butternut	Orange	Walnut

SPICES AND HERBS

Allspice: Cinnamon, ginger, nutmeg flavor; used in breads, pastries, jellies, jams, pickles.

Anise: Licorice flavor; used in candies, breads, fruit, wine, liqueurs.

Cinnamon: Pungent, sweet flavor; used in pastries, breads, pickles, wine, beer, liqueurs.

Clove: Pungent, sweet flavor; used for ham, sauces, pastries, puddings, fruit, wine, liqueurs.

Coriander: Butter-lemon flavor; used for cookies, cakes, pies, puddings, fruit, wine and liqueur punches.

Ginger: Strong, pungent flavor; used in anything sweet, plus with beer, brandy, liqueurs.

Nutmeg: Sweet, nutty flavor; used in pastries, puddings, vegetables.

Woodruff: Sweet vanilla flavor; used in wines, punches.

CANDY

Moulded Candies

¼ c.	solid white shortening	60 mL
2 T.	water	30 mL
1 c.	Powdered Sugar Replacement (p. 134)	250 mL

Beat shortening and water until fluffy; stir in sugar replacement. Knead until smooth. Continue as follows for individual moulds.

APPLES: Flavor with 2 t. (10 mL) unsweetened drink mix. Mould into apple shapes; brush lightly with diluted red food color. Use whole clove for stem.

BANANA: Flavor with 1 t. (5 mL) banana oil and knead in 3 drops of yellow food color. Mould into banana shapes.

ORANGE: Flavor with 1 t. (5 mL) orange oil and knead in 2 drops of red and 1 drop of yellow food color. Mould into orange shapes. Use whole clove for stem.

STRAWBERRY: Flavor with 2 t. (10 mL) strawberry flavoring or rose water and knead in 3 drops of red food color or desired amount. Mould into strawberry shapes, pricking each with toothpick to create seed holes. Push small green satin decoration into top for stem. (Satin decorations can be purchased at craft stores.)

Yield: 20 moulded fruits
Exchange 1 fruit: ⅓ fruit
                                ½ fat
Calories 1 fruit: 36

Butter Rum Patties

5 c.	puffed rice (unsweetened)	1250 mL
3 T.	granulated sugar replacement	45 mL
2	egg whites	2
2 t.	butter rum flavoring	10 mL
1 t.	vanilla extract	5 mL

Pour rice into blender and work into a powder. Pour into large bowl or food processor and add remaining ingredients. Work with wooden spoon or steel blade until mixture is completely blended; mixture will be sticky. Form into 20 patties. Place patties on an ungreased cookie sheet and bake at 300 °F (150 °C) for 15 to 20 minutes, or until surface feels dry.

Yield: 20 patties
Exchange 1 patty: ⅕ bread
Calories 1 patty: 23

Cream Cheese Mints

3-oz. pkg.	cream cheese (softened)	90-g pkg.
1 c.	Powdered Sugar Replacement (p. 134)	250 mL
2 T.	water	30 mL
½ to 1 t.	mint flavoring	2 to 5 mL
	food color as desired	

Beat cream cheese until fluffy. Stir in sugar replacement, water, flavoring and food color. (Dough may be divided into parts and different flavorings and food color added to each part.) Knead or work with the hand until dough is smooth. Roll into small marble-size balls, press each ball firmly into cavity of mould, and unmould onto waxed paper.

Yield: 60 pieces
Exchange 5 pieces: ⅓ fruit
　　　　　　　　½ fat
Calories 5 pieces: 50

Butter Mints

¼ c.	margarine (soft)	60 mL
2 T.	evaporated milk	30 mL
1 t.	butter flavoring	5 mL
1 c.	Powdered Sugar Replacement (p. 134)	250 mL

Cream together margarine, milk and butter flavoring until fluffy. Stir in sugar replacement. Knead or work with hands until smooth, roll into small marble-size balls and press each ball firmly into mould. Unmould onto waxed paper.

Yield: 45 pieces
Exchange 3 pieces: ⅓ low-fat milk
Calories 3 pieces: 56

Semisweet Dipping Chocolate

1 c.	nonfat dry milk powder	250 mL
⅓ c.	cocoa	90 mL
2 T.	paraffin wax	30 mL
½ c.	water	125 mL
1 T.	liquid shortening	15 mL
1 T.	liquid sugar replacement	15 mL

Combine milk powder, cocoa and wax in food processor or blender; blend to soft powder. Pour into top of double boiler and add water, stirring to blend. Add liquid shortening. Place over hot (not boiling) water, and cook and stir until wax pieces are completely dissolved and mixture is thick, smooth and creamy. Remove from heat. Stir in sugar replacement and let cool slightly. Dip candies according to recipe. Shake off excess chocolate. Place on very lightly greased waxed paper and allow to cool completely. (If candies do not remove easily, slightly warm the waxed paper over electric burner or with clothes iron.) Store in a cool place.

Yield: 1 c. (250 mL)
Exchange full recipe: 3 low-fat milk
Calories full recipe: 427

Chocolate Butter Creams

3-oz. pkg.	cream cheese (softened)	90-g pkg.
2 T.	skim milk	30 mL
1½ t.	white vanilla extract	7 mL
1 c.	Powdered Sugar Replacement (p. 134)	250 mL
1 recipe	Semisweet Dipping Chocolate (p. 15)	1 recipe

Beat cream cheese, milk and vanilla until fluffy; stir in powdered sugar replacement. Form into 30 balls and dip each one in chocolate.

Yield: 30 creams
Exchange 1 cream: ¼ low-fat milk
Calories 1 cream: 31

Fudge Candy

13-oz. can	evaporated skimmed milk	385-mL can
3 T.	cocoa	45 mL
¼ c.	butter	60 mL
1 T.	granulated sugar replacement	15 mL
dash	salt	dash
1 t.	vanilla extract	5 mL
2½ c.	unsweetened cereal crumbs	625 mL
¼ c.	nuts (very finely chopped)	60 mL

Combine milk and cocoa in saucepan; cook and beat over low heat until cocoa is dissolved. Add butter, sugar replacement, salt and vanilla. Bring to a boil; reduce heat and cook for 2 minutes. Remove from heat; add cereal crumbs and work in with wooden spoon. Cool 15 minutes. Divide in half; roll each half into a tube, 8 in. (20 cm) long. Roll each tube in finely chopped nuts. Wrap in waxed paper; chill overnight. Cut into ¼-in. (8 mm) slices.

Yield: 64 slices
Exchange 2 slices: ½ bread
                             ½ fat
Calories 2 slices: 60

Double Fudge Balls

⅓ c.	margarine (soft)	90 mL
3 T.	evaporated skimmed milk	45 mL
dash	salt	dash
1 t.	vanilla extract	5 mL
¼ c.	cocoa	60 mL
1 c.	Powdered Sugar Replacement (p. 134)	250 mL
1 recipe	Semisweet Dipping Chocolate (p. 15)	1 recipe

Cream together margarine, milk, salt and vanilla until fluffy. Stir in cocoa and sugar replacement. Knead or work with hands until dough is smooth, and form dough into 60 small balls. Dip balls in chocolate, cool completely; dip again and cool.

Yield: 60 balls
Exchange 1 ball: ⅓ bread
                 ½ fat
Calories 1 ball: 50

Chocolate Crunch Candy

1 c.	nonfat dry milk powder	250 mL
½ c.	cocoa	125 mL
2 T.	liquid fructose	30 mL
3 T.	water	45 mL
1½ c.	chow mein noodles	375 mL

Combine milk powder and cocoa in food processor or blender, blending to a fine powder. Stir in fructose and water and beat until smooth and creamy. Slightly crush the chow mein noodles and fold them into chocolate mixture. Drop by teaspoonfuls onto waxed paper. Cool at room temperature.

Yield: 30 pieces
Exchange 1 piece: ⅕ bread
Calories 1 piece: 11

Chocolate-Coated Cherries

1 recipe	Butter Mints (p. 15)	1 recipe
30	Bing cherries (with pit and stem)	30
½ recipe	Semisweet Dipping Chocolate (p. 15)	½ recipe

Wrap Butter Mint dough around each cherry; chill slightly. Dip in chocolate and dry completely.

Yield: 30 cherries
Exchange 1 cherry: ⅕ bread
⅕ fat
Calories 1 cherry: 31

Dried Apple Snack

1   apple   1

Peel, core and slice apple very thinly. Place on cookie rack. Bake at 200 °F (100 °C) for 1 hour (soft and chewy); 1½ hours (very chewy); or 2 hours (crisp).

Yield: 1 serving
Exchange: 1 fruit
Calories: 20

Jell Jots

3 env.	unflavored gelatin	3 env.
½ c.	cold water	125 mL
1¾-oz. pkg.	lo-cal jelly pectin	49.6-g pkg.
1½ c.	water	375 mL
1 T.	liquid sugar replacement	15 mL
1½ t.	lemon juice	7 mL
1 t.	fruit oil	5 mL
	or	
2 t.	fruit flavoring	10 mL
	food color	
	flour or cornstarch	

Combine gelatin and ½ c. (125 mL) cold water in bowl, stirring to mix, and set aside. Combine pectin and 1½ c. (375 mL) water in saucepan; cook and stir over medium-high heat until boiling. Cook and stir 12 minutes longer and then remove from heat. Add soaked gelatin, stirring until gelatin completely dissolves. Add sugar replacement, lemon juice, fruit oil and food color; stir to mix. Using teaspoon, fill holes in prepared pan (see below) with this mixture. Allow to set completely. Remove jots to strainer; shake off excess flour or cornstarch. (If jot mixture becomes hard, reheat slightly to liquefy.)

TO PREPARE PAN: Half fill 13 × 9 × 2-in. (33 × 23 × 5-cm) pan with flour or cornstarch. Place a thimble on finger and make holes in flour to bottom of pan.

Yield: 150 pieces
Exchange 50 pieces: 1 bread
Calories 50 pieces: 80

Butter Sticks

7 large	shredded wheat biscuits	7 large
½ c.	crunchy peanut butter	125 mL
3 T.	granulated sugar replacement	45 mL
2	egg whites	2
1 T.	flour	15 mL
1 T.	water	15 mL
1 t.	baking powder	5 mL
1 t.	vanilla extract	5 mL
1 recipe	Semisweet Dipping Chocolate (p. 15)	1 recipe

Break biscuits into large bowl or food processor. Add peanut butter, sugar replacement, egg whites, flour, water, baking powder and vanilla. Work with wooden spoon or steel blade until mixture is completely blended; mixture will be sticky. Form into 16 sticks and place them on an ungreased cookie sheet. Bake at 400 °F (200 °C) for 10 minutes, or until surface feels hard. Remove; cool slightly. Dip in chocolate.

Yield: 16 sticks
Exchange 1 stick: ⅔ bread
Calories 1 stick: 115

Cookie Brittle

½ c.	margarine	125 mL
2 t.	vanilla extract	10 mL
1 t.	salt	5 mL
3 T.	granulated sugar replacement	45 mL
2 c.	flour (sifted)	500 mL
1 c.	semisweet chocolate chips	250 mL
½ c.	walnuts (chopped fine)	125 mL

Combine margarine, vanilla, salt and sugar replacement in mixing bowl or food processor; beat until smooth. Stir in flour, chocolate chips and walnuts. Press into ungreased 15 × 10-in. (39 × 25-cm) pan. Bake at 375 °F (190 °C) for 25 minutes. Remove from oven, score into 2 × 1-in. (5 × 2.5-cm) pieces and cool completely. Break into candy pieces.

Yield: 60 pieces
Exchange 1 piece: ½ fat
⅓ bread
Calories 1 piece: 48

Sugared Pecans

½ c.	water	250 mL
¼ c.	granulated sugar replacement	60 mL
¼ c.	granulated brown sugar replacement	60 mL
1 c.	pecan halves	250 mL

Combine water and sugar replacements in saucepan, stirring to dissolve. Bring to boil, and boil for 3 minutes. Stir in pecans until completely coated; remove pan from heat. Allow pecans to rest in sugar water for 2 to 3 minutes. Remove with slotted spoon and cool completely.

Yield: 1 c. (250 mL)
Exchange 1 serving: 1 fat
Calories 1 serving: 48

Orange Walnuts

1 t.	unflavored gelatin	5 mL
½ c.	orange juice	125 mL
¼ c.	granulated sugar replacement	60 mL
1 t.	orange rind	5 mL
½ t.	vanilla extract	2 mL
1 c.	walnut halves	250 mL

Sprinkle gelatin over orange juice; allow to rest 5 minutes to soften. Cook and stir over medium heat until gelatin is dissolved. Stir in sugar replacement and orange rind. Bring to a boil, boil for 2 minutes and remove from heat. Cool slightly. Stir in vanilla; stir in walnuts until completely coated. Allow walnuts to rest in juice 10 minutes. Remove with slotted spoon and cool completely.

Yield: 1 c. (250 mL)
Exchange 1 serving: 1 fat
Calories 1 serving: 50

Crunch Nuts

7 large	shredded wheat biscuits	7 large
3 T.	granulated sugar replacement	45 mL
2 t.	almond extract	10 mL
2	egg whites	2

Crumble biscuits into blender; work into a powder. Combine with remaining ingredients in large mixing bowl or food processor. Work with wooden spoon or steel blade until completely blended; mixture will be sticky. Cover and refrigerate 1 hour. Form into walnut-size balls, place on ungreased cookie sheet and bake at 400 °F (200 °C) for 10 minutes.

Yield: 40 pieces
Exchange 1 piece: ⅕ bread
Calories 1 piece: 17

Coconut Macaroons

1 c.	evaporated skimmed milk	250 mL
2 t.	granulated sugar replacement	10 mL
3 c.	unsweetened coconut (shredded)	750 mL

Combine milk and sugar replacement in large bowl, stirring until sugar replacement dissolves. Add coconut and stir until coconut is completely moistened. Drop by teaspoonfuls onto greased cookie sheets, 2 to 3 in. (5 to 7 cm) apart. Bake at 350 °F (175 °C) for 15 minutes, or until tops are lightly browned. Remove from pan immediately.

Yield: 48 drops
Exchange 1 drop: ⅕ fruit
                     ½ fat
Calories 1 drop: 31

Fruit Candy Bars

1 env.	unflavored gelatin	1 env.
¼ c.	water	60 mL
1 c.	dried apricots	250 mL
1 c.	raisins	250 mL
1 c.	pecans	250 mL
1 T.	flour	15 mL
2 T.	orange peel (grated)	30 mL
1 t.	rum extract	5 mL

Sprinkle gelatin over water; allow to soften for 5 minutes. Heat and stir until gelatin is completely dissolved. Combine apricots, raisins, pecans, flour and orange peel in blender or food processor, working until finely chopped. Add to gelatin mixture. Add rum extract and stir to completely blend. Line 8-in. (20-cm) square pan with plastic wrap or waxed paper. Spread fruit mixture evenly into pan, and set aside to cool completely until candy is firm. Turn out onto cutting board, cut into 24 bars and wrap individually.

Yield: 24 bars
Exchange 1 bar: 1 fruit
                    ½ fat
Calories 1 bar: 68

Out-of-Bounds Candy Bars

1¼ c.	unsweetened coconut	310 mL
½ c.	milk	125 mL
2 t.	unflavored gelatin	10 mL
1 t.	cornstarch	5 mL
1 t.	white vanilla extract	5 mL
1 recipe	Semisweet Dipping Chocolate (p. 15)	1 recipe

Combine ¼ c. (60 mL) of the coconut, the milk, gelatin and cornstarch in blender; blend until smooth. Pour into small saucepan, cook and stir over medium heat until slightly thickened. Remove from heat and stir in vanilla and remaining coconut. Form into 8 bars, allow to firm and cool completely and dip in chocolate.

Yield: 8 bars
Exchange 1 bar: ⅔ full-fat milk
              1 fat
Calories 1 bar: 133

Peanut Butter Bars

1 t.	unflavored gelatin	5 mL
¾ c.	cold milk	190 mL
½ c.	creamy peanut butter	125 mL
6	shredded wheat biscuits	6
1 recipe	Semisweet Dipping Chocolate (p. 15)	1 recipe

Soak gelatin in ¼ c. (60 mL) of the cold milk; set aside. Combine peanut butter and remaining milk in top of double boiler and place over hot (not boiling) water. Cook and stir until smooth. Add soaked gelatin, cook and stir until gelatin is completely dissolved and smooth. Place 1 shredded wheat biscuit in peanut butter mixture. Turn to coat both sides and place on very lightly greased waxed paper. Repeat with remaining biscuits. Allow to firm and cool; dip in chocolate.

Yield: 6 bars
Exchange 1 bar: 1½ full-fat milk
Calories 1 bar: 238

Peanut Bars

1 c.	buttermilk	250 mL
3 T.	flour	45 mL
¼ c.	granulated sugar replacement	60 mL
2 c.	puffed rice (unsweetened)	500 mL
1 c.	nonfat dry milk powder	250 mL
½ c.	peanuts (slightly chopped)	125 mL

Combine buttermilk, flour and sugar replacement in saucepan. Cook and stir over medium heat until very thick; cool. Pour puffed rice and dry milk powder in blender and work until a fine powder. Work rice mixture into thickened buttermilk until completely blended. Form into 8 bars and roll each bar in chopped peanuts. Cool completely.

Yield: 8 bars
Exchange 1 bar: 1 low-fat milk
Calories 1 bar: 115

COOKIES

Refrigerator Cookies

Chocolate-Nut Refrigerator Cookies

¼ c.	shortening	60 mL
1 T.	granulated brown sugar replacement	15 mL
1	egg	1
1-oz. sq.	unsweetened chocolate (melted)	30-g sq.
½ t.	vanilla extract	2 mL
2 T.	walnuts (finely ground)	30 mL
2 T.	sour milk	30 mL
1 T.	water	15 mL
1 c.	flour	250 mL
1 t.	baking powder	5 mL
dash	salt	dash

Cream together shortening and brown sugar replacement. Add egg; beat well. Add melted chocolate, vanilla, walnuts, sour milk and water; beat to mix thoroughly. Add flour, baking powder and salt, and beat to blend. Shape into a roll, 1½-in. (3.75-cm) in diameter. Wrap in plastic wrap or waxed paper. Refrigerate at least 2 hours or overnight. Cut into ¼-in. (6-mm)-thick slices and place on ungreased cookie sheet. Bake at 400 °F (200 °C) for 8 to 10 minutes.

Microwave: Place 6 to 8 cookies on waxed paper. Cook on Low for 3 to 4 minutes, or until tops are set. Cool.

Yield: 30 cookies
Exchange 1 cookie: ½ vegetable
  ½ fat
Calories 1 cookie: 33

Pecan Refrigerator Cookies

¼ c.	shortening (soft)	60 mL
1 t.	granulated brown sugar replacement	5 mL
1	egg	1
½ t.	vanilla extract	2 mL
2 T.	broken pecans	30 mL
1 c.	flour	250 mL
dash	salt	dash
1 t.	baking powder	5 mL
2 T.	water	30 mL

With electric mixer or food processor, cream together shortening and sugar replacement. Add egg and beat well. Add vanilla and pecans; mix slightly. Add flour, salt, baking powder and water, mixing well. Shape into a roll, 1½ in. (3.75 cm) in diameter. Wrap in plastic wrap or waxed paper and refrigerate overnight. Cut into ¼-in. (6-mm)-thick slices and place on ungreased cookie sheet. Bake at 375 °F (190 °C) for 8 to 10 minutes.

Yield: 30 cookies
Exchange 1 cookie: ⅓ fruit
⠀⠀⠀⠀⠀⠀⠀⠀⠀⠀⠀⠀⠀½ fat
Calories 1 cookie: 32

Cream Cheese Cookies

¼ c.	vegetable shortening	60 mL
¼ c.	cream cheese (softened)	60 mL
2 t.	granulated fructose	10 mL
1 t.	granulated sugar replacement	5 mL
1	egg	1
1 T.	water	15 mL
1 c.	flour	250 mL
½ t.	baking powder	2 mL
dash	salt	dash

Cream together shortening, cream cheese, fructose and sugar replacement. Add egg and water, beating well. Sift together flour, baking powder and salt, and add to creamed mixture. Mix until thoroughly blended. Shape into a roll, 1½ in. (3.75 cm) in diameter. Refrigerate at least 2 hours or overnight. Cut into thin slices and place on ungreased cookie sheets. Bake at 350 °F (175 °C) for 8 to 10 minutes.

Yield: 30 cookies
Exchange 2 cookies: ½ fruit
                    ½ fat
Calories 2 cookies: 74

Drop Cookies

Walnut Macaroons

2 c.	quick-cooking rolled oats (uncooked)	500 mL
2 T.	granulated sugar replacement	30 mL
¼ t.	salt	1 mL
2 t.	vanilla extract	10 mL
½ c.	liquid shortening	125 mL
1	egg (well beaten)	1
½ c.	walnuts (very finely chopped)	125 mL

Combine oats, sugar replacement, salt, vanilla and liquid shortening in medium mixing bowl. Stir to mix well. Cover and refrigerate overnight. Add beaten egg and chopped walnuts and stir to blend thoroughly. Pack a small amount of cookie mixture level into teaspoon. Pat out onto ungreased cookie sheet. Bake at 350 °F (175 °C) for 15 minutes.

Microwave: Place 6 to 8 cookies in circle on waxed paper. Cook on Low for 4 to 5 minutes.

Yield: 42 cookies
Exchange 1 cookie: 1 fat
Calories 1 cookie: 40

Brazil Nut Cookies

½ c.	margarine	125 mL
4 t.	granulated sugar replacement	20 mL
2	egg yolks	2
¼ c.	unsweetened pineapple juice	60 mL
½ c.	lemon rind (grated)	2 mL
¼ c.	Brazil nuts (finely ground)	60 mL
1 c.	flour	250 mL

Cream together margarine and sugar replacement. Beat in egg yolks and pineapple juice, and add lemon rind and nuts. Stir to mix well. Allow to rest at room temperature for at least 15 minutes. Stir in flour and blend thoroughly. Drop by teaspoonfuls on lightly greased cookie sheets and bake at 375 °F (190 °C) for 10 to 12 minutes.

Yield: 24 cookies
Exchange 1 cookie: ½ fruit
　　　　　　　　　1 fat
Calories 1 cookie: 67

Holiday Hickory Drops

⅓ c.	shortening (soft)	90 mL
¼ c.	granulated brown sugar replacement	60 mL
2	eggs	2
2 c.	cake flour	500 mL
2 t.	baking powder	10 mL
½ c.	skim milk	125 mL
1 t.	vanilla extract	5 mL
½ c.	hickory nuts (chopped fine)	125 mL

Cream together shortening and brown sugar replacement until fluffy. Beat in eggs, one at a time. Combine cake flour and baking powder in sifter, and add alternately with milk to the creamed mixture. Fold in vanilla and nuts. Drop by teaspoonfuls onto greased cookie sheets. Bake at 375 °F (190 °C) for 12 to 15 minutes.

Yield: 60 cookies
Exchange 1 cookie: ⅕ bread
　　　　　　　　　⅓ fat
Calories 1 cookie: 31

Peanut Butter Cookies

¼ c.	margarine	60 mL
¼ c.	creamy peanut butter	60 mL
2 T.	granulated brown sugar replacement	30 mL
1 T.	granulated sugar replacement	15 mL
1	egg	1
¼ c.	water	60 mL
1 t.	vanilla extract	5 mL
1½ c.	flour	375 mL
1 t.	baking soda	5 mL
½ t.	baking powder	2 mL

Cream together margarine, peanut butter and sugar replacements. Add egg, water and vanilla, beating until fluffy. Combine flour, baking soda and baking powder in sifter and sift dry ingredients into creamed mixture. Stir to blend completely. Chill thoroughly, at least 2 hours or overnight. Drop by teaspoonfuls onto lightly greased cookie sheets, 2 to 3 in. (5 to 7 cm) apart. Press flat with a floured bottom of a small glass. Bake at 375 °F (190 °C) for 12 to 15 minutes.

Yield: 42 cookies
Exchange 1 cookie: ⅓ bread
Calories 1 cookie: 34

Teatime Puffs

2	egg whites	2
¼ t.	salt	1 mL
2 T.	granulated sugar replacement	30 mL
½ c.	creamy peanut butter (softened)	125 mL

Beat egg whites and salt until frothy. Add sugar replacement, beating until mixture is stiff, and fold in peanut butter. Drop by teaspoonfuls onto lightly greased cookie sheets. Bake at 325 °F (165 °C) for 20 minutes.

Yield: 24 cookies
Exchange 2 cookies: ½ medium-fat meat
$\qquad\qquad\qquad$ ½ fat
Calories 2 cookies: 64

Lace Cookies

½ c.	boiling water	125 mL
2 c.	rolled oats	500 mL
1 T.	margarine	15 mL
1 T.	granulated sugar replacement or granulated fructose	15 mL
2	eggs	2
1 t.	vanilla extract	5 mL
2 t.	baking powder	10 mL
½ t.	salt	2 mL

Pour boiling water over rolled oats. Stir to mix and then cover. Cream together margarine and sugar replacement, add eggs and vanilla and beat until fluffy. Add baking powder and salt to wet oats, stirring to blend. Pour rolled oats into creamed mixture; mix thoroughly. Drop by teaspoonfuls onto lightly greased cookie sheets, 2 to 3 in. (5 to 7 cm) apart. Bake at 375 °F (190 °C) for 12 to 15 minutes.

Yield: 48 cookies
Exchange 2 cookies: ⅓ vegetable
Calories 2 cookies: 36

Orange Cookies

1 medium	orange	1 medium
½ c.	shortening	125 mL
2 T.	granulated sugar replacement or granulated fructose	30 mL
1	egg	1
2 c.	flour	500 mL
½ t.	baking powder	2 mL
½ t.	baking soda	2 mL
¼ t.	salt	1 mL
½ c.	buttermilk	125 mL

Juice and grate the rind of the orange; remove seeds from the juice. Cream together shortening and sugar replacement. Add egg, orange juice and grated orange rind, beating until light and fluffy. Combine flour, baking powder, baking soda and salt in sifter, and add alternately with buttermilk to creamed mixture. Stir to blend. Drop by teaspoonfuls onto lightly greased cookie sheets, 2 to 3 in. (5 to 7 cm) apart. Bake at 375 °F (190 °C) for 10 to 12 minutes.

Yield: 60 cookies
Exchange 1 cookie with sugar replacement: ⅓ fruit
⅓ fat
Calories 1 cookie with sugar replacement: 27
Exchange 1 cookie with fructose: ⅓ fruit
⅓ fat
Calories 1 cookie with fructose: 30

Applesauce Cookies

¼ c.	margarine	60 mL
1T.	granulated sugar replacement	15 mL
½ c.	unsweetened applesauce	125 mL
2 T.	water	30 mL
1 c.	flour	250 mL
½ t.	baking soda	2 mL
½ t.	cinnamon	2 mL
¼ t.	salt	1 mL
¼ t.	cloves (ground)	1 mL
¼ c.	raisins (chopped)	60 mL

Cream together margarine and sugar replacement. Add applesauce and water, stirring to mix well. Combine flour, baking soda, cinnamon, salt and cloves in sifter. Sift dry ingredients into applesauce mixture; stir to blend. Fold in raisins. Drop by teaspoonfuls onto lightly greased cookie sheet. Bake at 375 °F (190 °C) for 10 to 12 minutes.

Microwave: Place 6 to 8 cookies on waxed paper. Cook on Low for 3 to 4 minutes, or until tops are set.

Yield: 30 cookies
Exchange 1 cookie: ½ fruit
⅕ fat
Calories 1 cookie: 33

Coconut Cookies

½ c.	margarine	125 mL
2 T.	granulated brown sugar replacement	30 mL
1	egg	1
¼ c.	water	60 mL
1 t.	vanilla extract	5 mL
1½ c.	flour (sifted)	375 mL
½ t.	baking soda	2 mL
½ t.	cream of tartar	2 mL
¾ c.	coconut (grated)	190 mL

Cream together margarine and brown sugar replacement. Beat in egg, water and vanilla until fluffy. Add flour, baking soda and cream of tartar, beating until smooth. Fold in coconut until completely blended. Drop by teaspoonfuls onto lightly greased cookie sheet. Bake at 375 °F (190 °C) for 10 to 12 minutes.

Microwave: Place 6 to 8 cookies on waxed paper. Cook on Low for 3 to 4 minutes, or until tops are set.

Yield: 42 cookies
Exchange 1 cookie: ⅓ fruit
⁣ ½ fat
Calories 1 cookie: 47

Chocolate-Coconut Drops

⅓ c.	margarine	90 mL
2T.	granulated brown sugar replacement	30 mL
1 t.	vanilla extract	5 mL
2	eggs	2
1½ c.	flour	375 mL
½ c.	cocoa	125 mL
½ t.	salt	2 mL
1 t.	baking soda	5 mL
⅓ c.	skim milk	90 mL
½ c.	unsweetened coconut (grated)	125 mL

Cream together margarine and brown sugar replacement. Beat in vanilla and eggs until light and fluffy. Sift flour, cocoa, salt and baking soda together; add alternately with milk to creamed mixture. Stir until well blended. Fold in coconut. Drop by teaspoonfuls onto lightly greased cookie sheets. Bake at 375 °F (190 °C) for 10 to 12 minutes.

Microwave: Place 6 to 8 cookies on waxed paper. Cook on Low for 3 to 4 minutes, or until tops are set. Cool.

Yield: 40 cookies
Exchange 1 cookie: ⅕ bread
                         ½ fat
Calories 1 cookie: 39

Hermit Cookies

½ c.	shortening	125 mL
3 T.	granulated brown sugar replacement	45 mL
1	egg	1
1½ c.	flour (sifted)	375 mL
1 t.	baking powder	5 mL
1 t.	cinnamon	5 mL
¼ t.	salt	1 mL
¼ t.	baking soda	1 mL
¼ t.	nutmeg	1 mL
¼ t.	cloves (ground)	1 mL
⅓ c.	skim milk	90 mL
⅓ c.	raisins (chopped)	90 mL
¼ c.	walnuts (chopped)	60 mL

Cream together shortening and brown sugar replacement. Add egg; beat until light and fluffy. Combine flour, baking powder, cinnamon, salt, baking soda, nutmeg and cloves in sifter; add alternately with milk to creamed mixture. Fold in raisins and walnuts. Drop by teaspoonfuls onto lightly greased baking sheets, 2 to 3 in. (5 to 7 cm) apart. Bake at 350 °F (175 °C) for 12 to 15 minutes.

Yield: 48 cookies
Exchange 1 cookie: ⅓ fruit
                         ½ fat
Calories 1 cookie: 40

Fruit Cookies

½ c.	margarine	60 mL
4 t.	granulated sugar replacement	20 mL
2	eggs	2
2 c.	flour (sifted)	500 mL
½ t.	baking soda	2 mL
¼ t.	salt	1 mL
½ t.	nutmeg	2 mL
¼ c.	hot apple juice	60 mL
¼ c.	raisins (chopped)	60 mL
¼ c.	currants	60 mL

Cream together margarine and sugar replacement. Add eggs; beat until fluffy. Combine flour, baking soda, salt and nutmeg in sifter; add alternately with hot apple juice to creamed mixture. Fold in raisins and currants. Allow to rest 15 minutes. Drop by teaspoonfuls onto lightly greased cookie sheet, 2 to 3 in. (5 to 7 cm) apart. Bake at 350 °F (175 °C) for 12 to 15 minutes.

Yield: 60 cookies
Exchange 1 cookie: ½ fruit
Calories 1 cookie: 27

Banana Cookies

¼ c.	margarine (soft)	60 mL
1 medium	banana	1 medium
1 t.	vanilla extract	5 mL
1	egg	1
1 T.	liquid fructose	15 mL
1 t.	baking powder	5 mL
dash	salt	dash
1½ c.	flour	375 mL

Combine margarine, banana, vanilla, egg and fructose in mixing bowl. Beat until smooth. Add baking powder, salt and flour, mixing to blend well. Drop by teaspoonfuls onto lightly greased cookie sheets. Bake at 375 °F (190 °C) for 8 to 10 minutes.

Yield: 40 cookies
Exchange 1 cookie: ½ fruit, ⅓ fat
Calories 1 cookie: 32

Cornflake Cookies

2	egg whites	2
½ t.	salt	2 mL
1 t.	white vinegar	5 mL
1 t.	vanilla extract	5 mL
2 t.	granulated sugar replacement	10 mL
1 t.	liquid fructose	5 mL
2½ c.	unsweetened cornflakes (crushed)	625 mL

Beat egg whites until frothy. Add salt and continue beating until stiff. Beat in vinegar, vanilla, sugar replacement and liquid fructose; lightly fold in cornflakes. Drop by teaspoonfuls onto greased cookie sheets, 2 to 3 in. (5 to 7 cm) apart. Bake at 350 °F (175 °C) for 12 to 15 minutes, or until lightly browned.

Yield: 42 cookies
Exchange 3 cookies: ⅓ fruit
Calories 3 cookies: 21

Cinnamon Cookies

2	eggs	2
2 T.	water	30 mL
5 t.	granulated sugar replacement	25 mL
1 t.	cinnamon	5 mL
1½ c.	flour	375 mL
½ t.	baking soda	2 mL
¼ t.	salt	1 mL

Beat eggs and water until light and fluffy. Beat in sugar replacement and cinnamon. Combine flour, baking soda and salt in sifter; sift half of the dry ingredients over egg mixture. Fold to completely blend. Repeat with remaining dry ingredients. Drop by teaspoonfuls onto greased cookie sheets, 2 to 3 inches (1 cm) apart. Bake at 375 °F (190 °C) for 10 to 12 minutes.

Yield: 20 cookies
Exchange 1 cookie: ½ bread
Calories 1 cookie: 41

Carrot Cookies

½ c.	margarine	125 mL
1 T.	granulated brown sugar replacement	15 mL
2 t.	granulated sugar replacement	10 mL
1	egg	1
2 T.	water	30 mL
1 t.	vanilla extract	5 mL
1 c.	cooked carrots (mashed)	250 mL
2 c.	flour	500 mL
½ t.	salt	2 mL
2 t.	baking powder	10 mL

Cream together margarine and sugar replacements. Add egg, water and vanilla, beating until light and fluffy, and beat in carrots. Combine flour, salt and baking powder in sifter. Sift dry ingredients into carrot mixture; stir to blend completely. Drop by teaspoonfuls onto lightly greased cookie sheets. Bake at 375 °F (190 °C) for 10 to 12 minutes.

Microwave: Place 6 to 8 cookies on waxed paper. Cook on Low for 3 to 4 minutes, or until tops are set.

Yield: 50 cookies
Exchange 1 cookie: ½ vegetable
Calories 1 cookie: 35

Chocolate Chip Cookies

¼ c.	margarine	60 mL
1 T.	granulated fructose	15 mL
1	egg	1
3 T.	water	45 mL
1 t.	vanilla extract	5 mL
¾ c.	flour	190 mL
¼ t.	baking soda	1 mL
¼ t.	salt	1 mL
½ c.	small semisweet chocolate chips	125 mL

Cream together margarine and fructose; beat in egg, water and vanilla. Combine flour, baking soda and salt in sifter. Sift dry ingredients into creamed mixture, stirring to blend thoroughly. Stir in chocolate chips. Drop by teaspoonfuls onto lightly greased cookie sheet, 2 in. (5 cm) apart. Bake at 375 °F (190 °C) for 8 to 10 minutes.

Yield: 30 cookies
Exchange 1 cookie: ½ fruit, ½ fat
Calories 1 cookie: 41

Christmas Melt-Aways

3	egg whites (beaten stiff)	3
2 T.	granulated sugar replacement	30 mL
	or granulated fructose	
½ t.	cream of tartar	2 mL
¼ t.	salt	1 mL
2 t.	green mint flavoring	10 mL

Beat sugar replacement, cream of tartar, salt and flavoring into egg whites. Drop by teaspoonfuls onto lightly greased cookie sheets. Bake at 325 °F (165 °C) for 10 minutes. Remove from pan right away.

Yield: 36 cookies
Exchange 6 cookies with sugar replacement: Negligible
Calories 6 cookies with sugar replacement: 10
Exchange 6 cookies with fructose: ⅕ fruit
Calories 6 cookies with fructose: 22

Cotton Candy Cookies

3	egg whites (beaten stiff)	3
2 T.	granulated sugar replacement	30 mL
	or granulated fructose	
2 t.	orange oil (or your favorite oil)	10 mL
1 t.	orange rind (grated)	5 mL

Beat sugar replacement, orange oil and rind into the stiff egg whites. Drop onto lightly greased cookie sheets. Bake at 325 °F (165 °C) for 8 to 10 minutes. Remove from pan immediately.

Yield: 36 cookies
Exchange 6 cookies with sugar replacement: Negligible
Calories 6 cookies with sugar replacement: 10
Exchange 6 cookies with fructose: ⅕ fruit
Calories 6 cookies with fructose: 22

Walnut Kisses

3	egg whites (beaten stiff)	3
2 T.	granulated sugar replacement or granulated fructose	30 mL
2 T.	cake flour (sifted)	30 mL
⅓ c.	walnuts (chopped fine)	90 mL
½ t.	vanilla extract	2 mL

Beat sugar replacement into stiff egg whites. Sprinkle flour over egg white mixture; gently fold flour into egg whites with wire whisk or wooden spoon. Fold in walnuts and vanilla. Drop by teaspoonfuls onto lightly greased cookie sheets. Bake at 325 °F (165 °C) for 10 minutes. Remove from pan immediately.

Yield: 36 cookies
Exchange 6 cookies with sugar replacement: ⅓ milk
Calories 6 cookies with sugar replacement: 63
Exchange 6 cookies with fructose: ½ milk
Calories 6 cookies with fructose: 78

Popcorn Drops

2 c.	unsalted popped corn	500 mL
3	egg whites	3
½ t.	baking powder	2 mL
¼ t.	salt	1 mL
¼ t.	cream of tartar	1 mL
2 T.	granulated sugar replacement	30 mL

Place popped corn in food processor or food grinder; grind into kernel-size pieces. Beat egg whites until frothy and add baking powder, salt and cream of tartar. Beat into stiff peaks. Add sugar replacement, beating until well blended. Fold popcorn pieces into stiffly beaten egg whites. Drop by teaspoonfuls onto lightly greased cookie sheets. Bake at 350 °F (175 °C) for 12 to 14 minutes, or until lightly browned.

Yield: 36 cookies
Exchange 6 cookies: Negligible
Calories 6 cookies: 16

Pineapple Drops

¼ c.	margarine	60 mL
1 T.	granulated brown sugar replacement	15 mL
1 T.	granulated sugar replacement	15 mL
1	egg	1
1 t.	pineapple flavoring	5 mL
1¼ c.	flour (sifted)	310 mL
½ t.	baking powder	2 mL
¼ t.	baking soda	1 mL
½ c.	unsweetened crushed pineapple (with juice)	125 mL

Cream together margarine and sugar replacements. Add egg and pineapple flavoring, beating until fluffy. Combine flour, baking powder and baking soda in sifter. Add alternately with crushed pineapple (and juice) to creamed mixture, mixing thoroughly. Drop by teaspoonfuls onto lightly greased cookie sheets, 2 to 3 in. (5 to 7 cm) apart. Bake at 375 °F (190 °C) for 10 to 12 minutes.

Yield: 36 cookies
Exchange 1 cookie: ⅓ fruit
Calories 1 cookie: 29

Bar Cookies

Chinese Chews

¾ c.	cake flour	190 mL
¾ t.	baking powder	4 mL
3 T.	granulated sugar replacement	45 mL
⅛ t.	salt	1 mL
1 c.	dates (finely chopped)	250 mL
1 c.	walnuts (finely chopped)	250 mL

Sift together cake flour, baking powder, sugar replacement and salt. Add dates and walnuts. Spread in well-greased 8-in. (20-cm) square pan. Bake at 350 °F (175 °C) for 40 minutes, or until done. Score into 1-in. (2.5-cm) squares while warm.

Yield: 64 cookies
Exchange 1 cookie: ⅓ bread
Calories 1 cookie: 24

Cherry Bars

CRUST:

1 c.	flour	250 mL
⅓ c.	butter	90 mL
2 T.	Powdered Sugar Replacement (p. 134)	30 mL

Combine ingredients. Work with pastry blender or food processor until mixture is the texture of coarse crumbs. Press into bottom of 13 × 9-in. (33 × 23-cm) lightly greased cookie sheet. Bake at 350 °F (175 °C) for 12 to 15 minutes. Cool.

FILLING:

½ c.	sour cherries (fresh or well drained)	125 mL
2	eggs	2
¼ c.	granulated brown sugar replacement	60 mL
½ c.	unsweetened coconut (grated)	125 mL
2 T.	flour	30 mL
½ t.	baking powder	2 mL
½ t.	salt	2 mL
1 t.	vanilla extract	5 mL

Pit and chop cherries. Beat eggs, and stir in chopped cherries and remaining ingredients until well blended. Pour over baked crust, spreading evenly. Bake at 350 °F (175 °C) for 25 minutes, or until set. Cool slightly. While warm, cut into 48 bars with a sharp knife.

Yield: 48 cookies
Exchange 2 cookies: ⅓ bread, 1 fat
Calories 2 cookies: 62

Dream Bars

CRUST:

⅓ c.	margarine (soft)	90 mL
¼ c.	granulated brown sugar replacement	60 mL
1 c.	flour	250 mL

Combine all ingredients in pastry blender or food processor until crumbly. Pat into 13 × 9-in. (33 × 23-cm) cookie pan. Bake at 375 °F (175 °C) for 10 minutes. Remove and cool.

2	eggs	2
¼ c.	granulated brown sugar replacement	60 mL
2 T.	flour	30 mL
1 t.	baking powder	5 mL
¼ t.	salt	2 mL
1 t.	vanilla extract	5 mL
1 T.	water	15 mL
⅔ c.	unsweetened coconut (grated)	190 mL
½ c.	walnuts (chopped fine)	125 mL

Beat eggs and stir in remaining ingredients until well blended. Pour over baked crust, spreading evenly. Bake at 375 °F (190 °C) for 20 minutes, or until set. Cool slightly. Cut into 48 bars with a sharp knife.

Yield: 48 cookies
Exchange 1 cookie: ⅕ bread, ⅕ fat
Calories 1 cookie: 37

Brownies

½ t.	baking powder	2 mL
½ t.	salt	2 mL
3 oz.	unsweetened chocolate (melted)	90 g
½ c.	shortening (soft)	125 mL
2	eggs (beaten)	2
2 T.	granulated sugar replacement	30 mL
1½ c.	flour	375 mL
1 t.	vanilla extract	5 mL

Combine all ingredients and beat vigorously until well blended. Spread mixture into greased 8-in. (20-cm) square pan. Bake at 350 °F (175 °C) for 30 to 35 minutes. Cut into 2-in. (5-cm) squares.

Microwave: Cook on Medium for 8 to 10 minutes, or until puffed and dry on top. Cut into 2-in. (5-cm) squares.

Yield: 16 brownies
Exchange 1 brownie: 1½ bread, 1½ fat
Calories 1 brownie: 136

Pumpkin Bars

⅓ c.	margarine	90 mL
¼ c.	granulated brown sugar replacement	60 mL
1	egg	1
2 T.	water	30 mL
½ c.	unsweetened pumpkin puree	125 mL
1½ c.	flour	325 mL
1 t.	allspice	5 mL

Cream margarine until fluffy. Add brown sugar replacement, egg and water, beating until completely blended. Beat in pumpkin puree, stir in flour and allspice, and mix to completely blend. Spread evenly in greased 13 × 9-in. (33 × 23-cm) cookie sheet. Bake at 350 °F (175 °C) for 16 to 18 minutes, or until sides pull away from pan. Cool and cut into bars.

Yield: 48 cookies
Exchange 2 cookies: ⅓ bread, ½ fat
Calories 2 cookies: 52

Toffee Squares

½ c.	margarine	125 mL
3 T.	granulated sugar replacement	45 mL
2	eggs	2
2 T.	water	30 mL
2 c.	flour	500 mL
1 t.	cinnamon	5 mL
1	egg white (slightly beaten)	1
½ c.	pecans (chopped fine)	125 mL

Cream margarine and sugar replacement until fluffy. Beat in whole eggs, one at a time. Add water, flour and cinnamon, mixing thoroughly. Spread into well-greased 15 × 10-in. (39 × 25-cm) cookie sheet. Pat with hand to level the surface. Brush beaten egg white over entire surface, and sprinkle evenly with chopped pecans. Slightly press pecans into cookie dough. Bake at 300 °F (150 °C) for 40 to 45 minutes, or until done. Cut into 1½-in. (3.75-cm) squares.

Yield: 72 cookies
Exchange 2 cookies: ⅓ bread, 1 fat
Calories 2 cookies: 60

Shaped Cookies

Rosettes

2	eggs	2
1 t.	granulated sugar replacement	5 mL
¼ t.	salt	1 mL
1 c.	skim milk	250 mL
2 t.	vanilla extract	10 mL
1 c.	flour	250 mL
	oil for deep-fat frying	
⅓ c.	Powdered Sugar Replacement (p. 134)	90 mL

Combine eggs, granulated sugar replacement and salt in mixing bowl and beat very slightly. Beat in milk, vanilla and flour until smooth. Heat deep fat to 365 °F (180 °C); heat rosette iron. Shake off excess oil. Dip into batter to within ¼ in. (8 mm) of top of iron. Return to hot oil; completely cover iron with oil. Fry 20 seconds or until golden brown. Remove rosette onto absorbent paper. When cool, dust sifted powdered sugar replacement over rosettes.

Yield: 40 cookies
Exchange 2 cookies: ⅓ bread
Calories 2 cookes: 32

Fattegmand

2	eggs	2
1 T.	granulated sugar replacement	15 mL
3 T.	evaporated skimmed milk	45 mL
¼ t.	salt	1 mL
2 c.	flour	500 mL
	oil for deep-fat frying	

Combine all ingredients, except oil; mix just until blended. Roll out on lightly floured surface and form into 70 thin strips. Fry in deep fat, heated to 365 °F (180 °C), until golden brown. Remove to absorbent paper.

Yield: 70 cookies
Exchange 2 cookies: ⅓ bread
Calories 2 cookies: 28

Spiced Pressed Cookies

⅓ c.	shortening (soft)	90 mL
3 T.	granulated sugar replacement	45 mL
1½ t.	vanilla extract	7 mL
3 T.	water	45 mL
3	eggs	3
2½ c.	cake flour	625 mL
3 t.	baking powder	15 mL
2 t.	cinnamon	10 mL
1 t.	nutmeg	5 mL
½ t.	clove (ground)	2 mL

Combine shortening and sugar replacement in mixing bowl; beat until light and fluffy. Combine vanilla, water and eggs in measuring cup, beating until blended. Combine cake flour, baking powder and spices in sifter. Sift flour mixture alternately with egg mixture into shortening. Blend well after each addition. Chill thoroughly (at least 2 hours). With cookie press, press into shapes on ungreased cookie sheet. Bake at 425 °F (220 °C) for 7 to 8 minutes. Remove from pan immediately.

Yield: 60 cookies
Exchange 1 cookie: ⅕ bread
⅓ fat
Calories 1 cookie: 27

Cookie Sticks

⅓ c.	butter (soft)	90 mL
3 T.	granulated sugar replacement	45 mL
3	eggs	3
¼ c.	water	60 mL
1 t.	almond extract	5 mL
3 c.	cake flour	750 mL
½ t.	baking soda	2 mL
½ t.	salt	2 mL
⅓ c.	Powdered Sugar Replacement (p. 134)	90 mL

Combine butter and granulated sugar replacement in mixing bowl, and beat until fluffy and lemon-colored. Combine eggs, water and almond extract in measuring cup, beating until well blended. Combine cake flour, baking soda and salt in sifter. Sift flour mixture alternately with egg mixture into butter. Blend well after each addition. Force dough through pastry tube onto an ungreased cookie sheet to make 1 × 2 in. (2.5 × 5 cm) sticks. Bake at 400 °F (200 °C) for 10 to 12 minutes. Remove from pan immediately; cool. Dust with powdered sugar replacement.

Yield: 50 cookies
Exchange 1 cookie: ⅓ bread
⅓ fat
Calories 1 cookie: 36

Peanut-Butter Fingers

1 c.	flour	250 mL
¼ t.	baking soda	1 mL
1½ t.	baking powder	7 mL
¼ t.	salt	1 mL
½ c.	solid shortening (soft)	125 mL
½ c.	peanut butter	125 mL
2 t.	orange rind (grated)	10 mL
2 T.	granulated brown sugar replacement	30 mL
1 T.	granulated sugar replacement	15 mL
1	egg	1

Sift together flour, baking soda, baking powder and salt. Beat shortening and peanut butter until creamy. Add orange rind, sugar replacements and egg to creamed mixture; beat until light and fluffy. Add flour mixture, stirring to blend well. Shape level tablespoonfuls into 2-in. (5-cm) fingers and place on ungreased cookie sheet. Bake at 350 °F (175 °C) for 12 to 15 minutes.

Microwave: Place 6 to 8 fingers on waxed paper and bake on Low for 5 to 6 minutes.

Yield: 48 cookies
Exchange 1 cookie: ⅓ fruit
½ fat
Calories 1 cookie: 43

Chocolate Tea Cookies

¼ c.	shortening (soft)	60 mL
3 T.	granulated sugar replacement	45 mL
1	egg	1
½ t.	vanilla extract	2 mL
2 T.	skim milk	30 mL
1¼ c.	cake flour (sifted)	310 mL
1-oz. sq.	unsweetened baking chocolate (melted)	28-g sq.

Cream shortening. Add sugar replacement, egg, vanilla and milk, blending well. Add half the sifted flour; mix to completely blend. Stir in melted chocolate and remaining flour. With cookie press, press onto ungreased cookie sheets. Bake at 350 °F (175 °C) for 20 to 22 minutes.

Yield: 36 cookies
Exchange 1 cookie: ⅕ bread, ⅓ fat
Calories 1 cookie: 32

Christmas Cutouts

½ c.	shortening (soft)	125 mL
3 T.	granulated sugar replacement	45 mL
1	egg	1
2½ c.	cake flour	625 mL
2 t.	baking powder	10 mL
½ t.	salt	2 mL
½ c.	skim milk	125 mL
2 T.	water	30 mL
1 t.	vanilla extract	5 mL

Cream shortening. Add sugar replacement and egg; beat well. Combine cake flour, baking powder and salt in sifter. Combine milk, water and vanilla in measuring cup. Sift flour mixture alternately with milk into creamed mixture, mixing well after each addition. Chill thoroughly. Roll out to 1/16-in. (1.5-mm) thickness on pastry cloth, cut with cookie cutter, and decorate.

Yield: One hundred 2-in. (5-cm) cookies
Exchange 3 cookies: ⅓ bread
Calories 3 cookies: 58

Walnut Party Cookies

½ c.	margarine (soft)	125 mL
2 T.	granulated sugar replacement	30 mL
dash	salt	dash
1 t.	vanilla extract	5 mL
1½ c.	cake flour (sifted)	375 mL
24	walnut halves	24

Combine margarine, sugar replacement, salt and vanilla in medium mixing bowl. Beat until light and fluffy. Stir in cake flour and refrigerate dough for at least 1 hour. Form dough into 24 small balls, place on ungreased cookie sheet and press walnut half into top of each cookie ball. Bake at 350 °F (175 °C) for 20 minutes, or until done.

Microwave: Place 6 to 8 cookie balls in circle on waxed paper; press walnut half into top of each. Cook on Low for 5 to 6 minutes.

Yield: 24 cookies
Exchange 1 cookie: ½ fruit, 1 fat
Calories 1 cookie: 55

Peanut-Butter Balls

1 c.	margarine (soft)	250 mL
2T.	granulated sugar replacement	30 mL
1 t.	vanilla extract	5 mL
2 T.	water	30 mL
2 c.	flour	500 mL
1	egg white (beaten)	1
½ c.	peanuts (very finely chopped)	125 mL

Beat margarine with sugar replacement until creamy. Add vanilla, water and flour, mixing well. Refrigerate 1 hour. Form into 1-in. (2.5-cm) balls, dip into beaten egg white and roll in chopped peanuts. Place on ungreased cookie sheets. Bake at 350 °F (175 °C) for 10 to 12 minutes.

Yield: 54 cookies
Exchange 1 cookie: ⅓ fruit, 1 fat
Calories 1 cookie: 56

Cinnamon Nut Balls

1¼ c.	flour	310 mL
1 t.	baking powder	5 mL
⅛ t.	salt	1 mL
½ c.	margarine (soft)	125 mL
3 T.	granulated sugar replacement	45 mL
1	egg (beaten)	1
1 t.	vanilla extract	5 mL
2 t.	cinnamon	10 mL
½ c.	walnuts (finely chopped)	125 mL

Sift together flour, baking powder and salt. Beat margarine, sugar replacement, egg and vanilla until creamy. Add flour mixture, stirring to mix completely. Refrigerate 1 hour. Shape level tablespoonfuls of cookie dough into balls and roll each one in mixture of cinnamon and walnuts. Place on greased cookie sheets 2 in. (5 cm) apart. Bake at 375 °F (190 °C) for 12 to 15 minutes. Remove from pan immediately.

Yield: 30 cookies
Exchange 1 cookie: ⅓ bread, 1 fat
Calories 1 cookie: 60

Kaiser Cookies

3 T.	margarine	45 mL
1 T.	granulated sugar replacement	15 mL
1 t.	vanilla extract	5 mL
1	egg	1
1 c.	flour (sifted)	250 mL
⅔ c.	water	160 mL

Beat margarine until fluffy. Add sugar replacement, vanilla and egg, beating until well blended. Add flour and water alternately to margarine mixture, beating to a thin batter. Lightly grease krumkake or kaiser iron. Place 1 T. (15 mL) of batter in center of iron, close lid, cook on both sides until golden brown, and remove from iron. Cool on rack.

Yield: 16 cookies
Exchange 1 cookie: ⅓ fruit, ½ fat
Calories 1 cookie: 50

Chocolate Wafers

¼ c.	margarine (soft)	60 mL
4 t.	granulated sugar replacement	20 mL
1	egg	1
2 T.	cocoa	30 mL
1 t.	vanilla extract	5 mL
1 c.	flour	250 mL
1 t.	baking powder	5 mL
¼ t.	baking soda	1 mL
dash	salt	dash
2 T.	water	30 mL

Combine margarine, sugar replacement, egg, cocoa and vanilla in mixing bowl or food processor. With electric mixer or steel blade, whip until creamy. Add flour, baking powder, baking soda, salt and water; mix well. Shape into balls. Wrap in waxed paper or plastic wrap. Chill at least 1 hour or overnight. Roll out dough to ⅛-in. (3-mm) thickness on lightly floured surface. Cut with 2½-in. (6.25-cm) round cookie cutter and place on ungreased cookie sheets. Bake at 350 °F (175 °C) for 8 to 10 minutes.

Yield: 30 wafers
Exchange 1 wafer: ⅓ vegetable
Calories 1 wafer: 29

GELATIN DESSERTS

Black Walnut Bavarian

1 env.	unflavored gelatin	1 env.
¼ c.	cold water	60 mL
3	egg yolks	3
2 T.	granulated sugar replacement or granulated fructose	30 mL
¼ t.	salt	1 mL
¾ c.	skim milk	190 mL
1 t.	vanilla extract	5 mL
½ c.	black walnuts (chopped fine)	125 mL
1 c.	lo-cal whipped topping (prepared)	250 mL

Combine gelatin and cold water in small cup; set aside 10 minutes to soften. Beat egg yolks, sugar replacement and salt in top of double boiler, and place top of double boiler over hot (not boiling) water. Stir in milk and cook over simmering water until mixture thickens; remove from heat. Stir in softened gelatin until completely dissolved, and add vanilla and black walnuts. Remove top of double boiler from heat and let cool completely. Fold in topping, spoon into serving dishes or mould, and chill thoroughly.

Yield: 6 servings
Exchange 1 serving with sugar replacement: ½ full-fat milk
1 fat
Calories 1 serving with sugar replacement: 129
Exchange 1 serving with fructose: ½ high-fat meat
⅓ fruit
1 fat
Calories 1 serving with fructose: 141

50

Maple Bavarian

1 env.	unflavored gelatin	1 env.
2 T.	cold water	30 mL
½ c.	lo-cal maple syrup	125 mL
3	egg yolks (beaten)	3
2 T.	granulated sugar replacement	30 mL
dash	salt	dash
¾ c.	skim milk	190 mL
1 t.	rum flavoring	5 mL
2 c.	lo-cal whipped topping (prepared)	500 mL

Sprinkle gelatin over cold water in small cup and set aside to soften. Combine maple syrup, beaten egg yolks, sugar replacement, salt and milk in top of double boiler. Cook and stir over simmering (not boiling) water until mixture thickens. (*Do not allow bottom of pan to touch water.*) Add softened gelatin, stir to dissolve completely, and remove from heat. Stir in rum flavoring. Remove top of double boiler from heat. When mixture has cooled completely, fold it into the topping. Scoop into serving dishes or mould; chill thoroughly.

Yield: 8 servings
Exchange 1 serving: ⅓ low-fat milk
Calories 1 serving: 76

Coconut Bavarian

1 env.	unflavored gelatin	1 env.
2 T.	cold water	30 mL
1½ c.	skim milk	375 mL
½ c.	unsweetened coconut	125 mL
1 t.	white vanilla extract	5 mL
1 c.	lo-cal whipped topping (prepared)	250 mL

Combine gelatin and cold water in small cup; set aside 10 minutes to soften. Combine milk and coconut in blender, whip on High for 2 minutes, and pour into saucepan. Stir and cook over low heat just to boiling, but *do not boil.* Remove from heat. Stir in softened gelatin, until completely dissolved, and add the vanilla. Cool completely and fold coconut mixture into topping.

Yield: 6 servings
Exchange 1 serving: ⅓ full-fat milk
Calories 1 serving: 64

Bavarian Deluxe

1 env.	unflavored gelatin	1 env.
2 T.	cold water	30 mL
4	egg yolks	4
2 T.	granulated sugar replacement	30 mL
dash	salt	dash
¼ c.	evaporated skim milk	60 mL
¼ c.	water	60 mL
1 env.	lo-cal whipped topping mix (prepared)	1 env.

Combine gelatin and 2 T. (30 mL) cold water in small cup; set aside 10 minutes to soften. Combine egg yolks, sugar replacement and salt in top of double boiler, beating with electric beater or wire whisk until well blended. Place top of double boiler over hot (not boiling) water, and beat in milk and ¼ c. (60 mL) water. Cook and stir over simmering water until mixture thickens, remove from heat, and stir in gelatin until dissolved. Remove top of double boiler from heat; cool until almost set. Fold egg mixture into topping, spoon into serving dishes or mould, and chill thoroughly.

Yield: 6 servings
Exchange 1 serving: ½ high-fat meat
                       1 fat
Calories 1 serving: 93

Quick Gelatin

1 qt.	cold water	1 L
2 env.	unflavored gelatin	2 env.
1 env.	any flavor unsweetened drink mix	1 env.
2 T.	granulated sugar replacement	30 mL

Sprinkle unflavored gelatin over 1 c. (250 mL) of the cold water and allow to rest 10 minutes to soften. Place over medium heat; bring to boil. Cook and stir until gelatin is completely dissolved. Combine drink mix, sugar replacement and remaining 3 c. (750 mL) of water in mixing bowl, stirring to blend. Add gelatin mixture and stir to blend completely. Refrigerate until firm.

Yield: 4 c. (1 L)
Exchange: Negligible
Calories: Negligible

Blueberry Snow

1 env.	unflavored gelatin	1 env.
¼ c.	cold water	60 mL
½ c.	boiling water	125 mL
2 c.	fresh blueberries (rinsed)	500 mL
1 t.	lemon juice	5 mL
2 T.	granulated sugar replacement	30 mL
2	egg whites (beaten stiff)	2
6	fresh strawberries	6

Sprinkle gelatin over cold water in mixing bowl; set aside 10 minutes to soften. Add boiling water and stir to completely dissolve. (If gelatin does not dissolve completely, heat slightly.) Set aside. Combine blueberries, lemon juice and sugar replacement in mixing bowl or food processor and whip into a puree. Stir completely into gelatin mixture. When blueberry mixture is cool, thick and syrupy, beat until frothy. Fold stiffly beaten egg whites into blueberry mixture. Spoon into 6 serving dishes; refrigerate until set. Before serving, top with fresh strawberries.

Yield: 6 servings
Exchange 1 serving: ⅓ fruit
Calories 1 serving: 18

Orange Gelatin

1 env.	unflavored gelatin	1 env.
2 T.	cold water	30 mL
½ c.	boiling water	125 mL
1 T.	liquid sugar replacement	15 mL
dash	salt	dash
1½ c.	unsweetened orange juice	375 mL
2 T.	lemon juice	30 mL

Sprinkle gelatin over cold water in small cup; set aside 10 minutes to soften. Combine boiling water and softened gelatin in 2-c. (500-mL) mixing bowl, stirring until gelatin is completely dissolved. Add sugar replacement, salt, orange juice and lemon juice; stir to completely blend. Refrigerate until set.

Yield: 6 servings
Exchange 1 serving: ½ fruit
Calories 1 serving: 30

Raspberry Dream

1 env.	unflavored gelatin	1 env.
2 T.	cold water	30 mL
½ c.	boiling water	125 mL
2 t.	liquid sugar replacement	10 mL
dash	salt	dash
3-oz. pkg.	cream cheese (softened)	90-g pkg.
3 c.	fresh raspberries	750 mL
	cold water	

Sprinkle gelatin over 2 T. (30 mL) cold water in small cup; set aside 10 minutes to soften. Combine boiling water and softened gelatin in mixing bowl, stirring until gelatin is completely dissolved. Add sugar replacement and salt and stir to blend. Beat cream cheese and 2 T. (30 mL) of gelatin mixture until creamy and then spoon cheese mixture into bottom of a 4-c. (1000-mL) wet mould. Refrigerate until set. Mash 2 c. (500 mL) of the raspberries, adding enough cold water to make 1½ c. (375 mL), and stir into remaining gelatin mixture. Refrigerate until consistency of egg whites. Fold in remaining cup (125 mL) whole raspberries, pour into mould over cream cheese and refrigerate until set. Unmould.

Yield: 6 servings
Exchange 1 serving: 1 fruit
                        1 fat
Calories 1 serving: 88

Lemon Bisque

1½ c.	graham cracker crumbs	375 mL
1 env.	lo-cal lemon gelatin	1 env.
1¼ c.	boiling water	310 mL
2 T.	lemon juice	30 mL
2 T.	granulated sugar replacement	30 mL
	or granulated fructose	
1 env.	lo-cal whipped topping mix (prepared)	1 env.
½ c.	walnuts (chopped fine)	125 mL

Spread graham cracker crumbs on bottom of 9-in. (23-cm) baking dish and press down to tighten crumbs; refrigerate. Dissolve lemon gelatin in boiling water and add lemon juice and sugar replacement. Chill mixture until congealed. Beat until fluffy. Fold lemon mixture and nuts into topping. Pour mixture into baking dish; refrigerate 3 hours or overnight.

Yield: 9 servings.
Exchange 1 serving with sugar replacement: 1 fruit
1 fat

Calories 1 serving with sugar replacement: 127
Exchange 1 serving with fructose: 1 fruit
1 fat

Calories 1 serving with fructose: 133

Lemon Snow

1 env.	unflavored gelatin	1 env.
¼ c.	cold water	60 mL
½ c.	boiling water	125 mL
3 T.	granulated sugar replacement or granulated fructose	45 mL
¼ c.	fresh lemon juice	60 mL
2 t.	fresh lemon rind (grated)	10 mL
3	egg whites (beaten stiff)	3

Sprinkle gelatin over cold water in mixing bowl; set aside for 10 minutes to soften. Add boiling water and stir until gelatin is completely dissolved, and add sugar replacement, lemon juice and rind. Stir to thoroughly blend. Cool until mixture is consistency of unbeaten egg whites. With an electric beater, whip lemon mixture until frothy. Fold beaten egg whites into lemon mixture. Spoon into 6 serving dishes; refrigerate until set.

Yield: 6 servings
Exchange 1 serving with sugar replacement: Negligible
Calories 1 serving with sugar replacement: 8
Exchange 1 serving with fructose: ½ fruit
Calories 1 serving with fructose: 26

Lemon Gelatin

1 env.	unflavored gelatin	1 env.
¼ c.	cold water	60 mL
1¼ c.	boiling water	375 mL
4 t.	liquid sugar replacement	20 mL
dash	salt	dash
⅓ c.	fresh lemon juice	90 mL
1 t.	fresh lemon rind (grated)	5 mL

Sprinkle gelatin over cold water in small cup; set aside 10 minutes to soften. Combine boiling water and softened gelatin in a 2-c. (500-mL) mixing bowl, stirring until gelatin is completely dissolved. Add sugar replacement, salt, lemon juice and rind; stir to completely blend. Refrigerate until set.

Yield: 2 c. (500 mL)
Exchange: Negligible
Calories: Negligible

Cranberry Charlotte

2 c.	vanilla wafer crumbs	500 mL
2 T.	margarine (melted)	30 mL
2 t.	water	10 mL
1 env.	unflavored gelatin	1 env.
1¼ c.	unsweetened cranberry juice	310 mL
2 T.	liquid sugar replacement	30 mL
3	egg whites (beaten stiff)	3
2 c.	lo-cal whipped topping (prepared)	500 mL

Combine wafer crumbs, melted margarine and water in mixing bowl or food processor, and work until well blended. Line the bottom and part of the sides of an 8-in. (20-cm) springform pan; refrigerate. Sprinkle gelatin over cranberry juice in small saucepan; set aside for 5 minutes to soften. Stir and cook over low heat until gelatin is completely dissolved. Remove from heat, cool slightly, and add sugar replacement. Chill until mixture is consistency of thick syrup. Beat until frothy. Fold in stiffly beaten egg whites and 1½ c. (375 mL) of the topping. Spoon into springform pan and refrigerate until firm, at least 6 hours. Remove springform sides carefully. Garnish with remaining topping.

Yield: 10 servings
Exchange 1 serving: ½ fat; **Calories 1 serving:** 47

Cranberry Cream

1 env.	unflavored gelatin	1 env.
1½ c.	unsweetened cranberry juice	375 mL
2 T.	granulated sugar replacement or granulated fructose	30 mL
dash	salt	dash
1 c.	lo-cal whipped topping (prepared)	250 mL

Combine gelatin and cranberry juice in saucepan and allow to sit 10 minutes, or until gelatin is softened. Cook and stir over medium heat until mixture boils and gelatin is completely dissolved. Remove from heat; stir in sugar replacement and salt. Cool till gelatin begins to set, fold into topping, and spoon into dishes. Refrigerate till set.

Yield: 6 servings
Exchange 1 serving with sugar replacement: ¼ fruit
Calories 1 serving with sugar replacement: 19
Exchange 1 serving with fructose: ½ fruit
Calories 1 serving with fructose: 31

Cranberry Gelatin Dessert

1 c.	fresh cranberries	250 mL
1½ c.	water	375 mL
2 T.	granulated sugar replacement	30 mL
1 env.	lo-cal cherry gelatin	1 env.
¾ c.	ice water	190 mL
1 c.	fresh or unsweetened orange slices	250 mL

Combine cranberries, 1½ c. (375 mL) water and sugar replacement in saucepan. Cook and stir over medium heat until cranberry skins have popped and mixture is slightly thickened. Remove from heat. Add gelatin and stir to completely dissolve. Add ice water, and cool mixture until it is the consistency of egg whites. Fold in orange slices, and pour mixture into serving dish or mould.

Yield: 4 servings
Exchange 1 serving: ¼ fruit; **Calories 1 serving:** 24

Charlotte Russe

1 env.	unflavored gelatin	1 env.
¼ c.	cold water	60 mL
½ c.	skim milk	125 mL
1 T.	granulated sugar replacement or granulated fructose	15 mL
2 t.	white vanilla extract	10 mL
2 c.	lo-cal whipped topping (prepared)	500 mL
six ¼-in. slices	Sponge Cake (p. 124)	six 8-mm slices

Sprinkle gelatin over cold water in small saucepan; set aside for 10 minutes to soften. Add milk, cooking and stirring over low heat until gelatin is completely dissolved. Remove from heat and cool slightly. Stir in sugar replacement and vanilla. Chill until mixture is consistency of unbeaten egg whites, fold in topping, and line 6 tart moulds with sponge-cake slices. Spoon topping mixture into moulds and refrigerate until firm. Unmould before serving.

Yield: 6 servings
Exchange 1 serving with sugar replacement: ½ fruit
                                                                    1 fat
Calories 1 serving with sugar replacement: 74
Exchange 1 serving with fructose: ½ fruit
                                                    1 fat
Calories 1 serving with fructose: 80

Christmas Gelatin Dessert

1 env.	unflavored gelatin	1 env.
3 T.	granulated sugar replacement	45 mL
1¼ c.	water	310 mL
5	egg whites	5
1 t.	almond extract	5 mL
1 t.	red food color	5 mL
1 t.	green food color	5 mL

Combine gelatin, sugar replacement and water in saucepan; cook and stir over medium heat until gelatin dissolves. Chill until partially set. Beat egg whites and almond extract into stiff peaks. Beat gelatin mixture until frothy and fold into egg whites. Divide mixture equally among 3 bowls. Tint one mixture pink, another light green, and leave the third one white. Spread pink mixture into bottom of rinsed 6-c. (1500-mL) mould. Add white layer, then the green layer. Chill at least 4 hours, or until completely set.

Yield: 10 servings
Exchange 1 serving: Negligible
Calories 1 serving: 6

Pecan Whip

1 env.	unflavored gelatin	1 env.
¼ c.	cold water	60 mL
3	eggs (separated)	3
2 T.	granulated sugar replacement	30 mL
dash	salt	dash
¾ c.	skim milk	190 mL
2 t.	vanilla extract	10 mL
½ c.	pecans (ground fine)	125 mL
½ t.	cream of tartar	2 mL

Sprinkle gelatin on top of water in small cup; set aside 10 minutes to soften. Beat egg yolks until frothy in top of double boiler. Add sugar replacement, salt and milk, beating well. Place top of double boiler over simmering (not boiling) water. (*Do not allow bottom of pan to touch water.*) Cook and stir until mixture coats spoon, and then stir in softened gelatin until it is completely dissolved. Stir in 1 t. (5 mL) of the vanilla and the pecans. Remove top of double boiler from heat and let cool completely. Combine egg whites, cream of tartar and remaining 1 t. (5 mL) of vanilla, beating until very stiff, and fold into cooled pecan mixture. Spoon into serving dishes.

Yield: 6 servings
Exchange 1 serving: ½ high-fat meat
                             ⅓ fruit
                             1 fat
Calories 1 serving: 112

Mocha Mounds

1 env.	unflavored gelatin	1 env.
2 T.	cold water	30 mL
1¼ c.	strong boiling coffee	310 mL
1-oz. sq.	bitter chocolate (melted)	30-g sq.
1 T.	liquid sugar replacement	15 mL
3	egg whites (beaten stiff)	3
8 T.	lo-cal whipped topping (prepared)	120 mL

Sprinkle gelatin over cold water in mixing bowl; set aside 10 minutes to soften. Add boiling coffee and stir to completely dissolve gelatin. Stir in melted chocolate and sugar replacement until completely blended. Cool mixture to consistency of unbeaten egg whites. With electric beater, beat mocha mixture until frothy. Fold stiffly beaten egg whites into the mixture. Spoon into 8 serving dishes; refrigerate until set. Before serving, top with 1 T. (15 mL) topping.

Yield: 8 servings
Exchange 1 serving: ½ fat
Calories 1 serving: 39

Peach Rice Dessert

6	peach halves (peeled)	6
½ c.	orange juice	125 mL
1½ t.	unflavored gelatin	7 mL
2 c.	cooked rice (cold)	500 mL
dash	salt	dash
1 c.	lo-cal whipped topping (prepared)	250 mL

Place each peach half in individual mould or custard cup. Combine orange juice and gelatin in saucepan, cooking over medium heat until gelatin is dissolved. Add cooked rice and salt, stirring to blend completely. Fold in topping, pour over peach halves, and chill until set. Unmould.

Yield: 6 servings
Exchange 1 serving: 2 fruit, ½ fat
Calories 1 serving: 122

Lemon Soufflé

1 env.	unflavored gelatin	1 env.
¼ c.	cold water	60 mL
½ c.	lemon juice	125 mL
3 T.	granulated sugar replacement	45 mL
2 t.	lemon rind	10 mL
3	egg whites (beaten stiff)	3
2 c.	lo-cal whipped topping (prepared)	500 mL

Sprinkle gelatin over cold water in saucepan and allow to soften for 10 minutes. Add lemon juice, and bring mixture to a boil. Cook and stir until gelatin is completely dissolved; remove from heat. Stir in sugar replacement and lemon rind. Refrigerate until completely cool and set to thick syrupy stage. Fold beaten egg whites, then the topping into gelatin mixture. Spoon into serving dish; refrigerate till set.

Yield: 8 servings
Exchange 1 serving: 1 fat
Calories 1 serving: 37

Bing Cherry Soufflé

1 env.	unflavored gelatin	1 env.
¾ c.	water	190 mL
2 c.	Bing cherries (pitted)	500 mL
1 T.	lemon juice	15 mL
2 T.	granulated sugar replacement	30 mL
3	egg whites (beaten stiff)	3
2 c.	lo-cal whipped topping (prepared)	500 mL

Sprinkle gelatin over water in saucepan and allow to soften for 10 minutes. Chop 1 c. (250 mL) of the cherries. Add cherries, lemon juice and sugar replacement to gelatin mixture, and bring to a boil. Cool and stir 5 minutes; refrigerate to thick syrup stage. Fold in remaining cherries. Thicken until firm but not solid. Fold in beaten egg whites, then the topping. Spoon into soufflé dish; refrigerate till set.

Yield: 8 servings
Exchange 1 serving: ½ fruit, 1 fat
Calories 1 serving: 58

Rhubarb Soufflé

1 qt.	rhubarb (chopped)	1 L
¼ c.	water	60 mL
¼ c.	granulated sugar replacement or granulated fructose	60 mL
1 t.	strawberry flavoring	5 mL
1 env.	unflavored gelatin	1 env.
2 T.	cold water	30 mL
3	egg whites	3
1 t.	vanilla extract	5 mL
2 c.	lo-cal whipped topping (prepared)	500 mL

Combine rhubarb and ¼ c. (60 mL) water in saucepan. Cook and stir over medium heat until rhubarb is very soft; remove from heat. Stir in sugar replacement and strawberry flavoring. Sprinkle gelatin over 2 T. (30 mL) cold water; set aside 10 minutes to soften. Stir gelatin into hot rhubarb until gelatin is completely dissolved. Set aside to completely cool. Beat egg whites and vanilla until very stiff and fold into cooled rhubarb mixture. Fold topping into rhubarb mixture. Fit a 2-in. (5-cm) waxed paper collar around a 1½-qt. (1½-L) soufflé dish. Spoon rhubarb mixture into dish. Refrigerate until set (at least 8 hours). Remove collar and serve.

Yield: 6 servings
Exchange 1 serving with sugar replacement: ⅓ lean meat
Calories 1 serving with sugar replacement: 50
Exchange 1 serving with fructose: ⅓ lean meat
                                        ½ fruit
Calories 1 serving with fructose: 70

PUDDINGS, CUSTARDS
AND CRÈMES

Hot Fudge Pudding

1 c.	flour	250 mL
3 T.	granulated sugar replacement	45 mL
½ t.	baking soda	2 mL
¼ t.	salt	1 mL
three 1-oz. sq.	bitter chocolate	three 30-g sq.
2 T.	white vinegar	30 mL
⅓ c.	skim milk	90 mL
2 T.	liquid shortening	30 mL
2 T.	granulated brown sugar replacement	30 mL
1¾ c.	boiling water	440 mL

Sift flour, granulated sugar replacement, baking soda and salt into medium mixing bowl. Melt 1 square of the bitter chocolate. Add vinegar, milk, shortening and the melted chocolate to flour mixture; stir to blend. Pour into well-greased 8-in. (20-cm) square baking dish, and sprinkle with brown sugar replacement. Add remaining chocolate to the boiling water; heat until chocolate is melted. Pour chocolate-water mixture over pudding batter, and bake at 350 °F (175 °C) for 45 minutes. Serve warm from baking dish.

Yield: 10 servings
Exchange 1 serving: 1 bread
                       1 fat
Calories 1 serving: 105

Vanilla Pudding

2 c.	low-fat milk (2% milkfat)	500 mL
2 T.	cornstarch	30 mL
1	egg (slightly beaten)	1
1 T.	liquid sugar replacement	15 mL
1 t.	vanilla extract	5 mL
2 t.	margarine (melted)	10 mL

Combine milk and cornstarch in saucepan. Cook and stir over medium heat until slightly thickened; remove from heat. Pour small amount of milk mixture into the beaten egg, stirring to blend. Pour egg-milk mixture back into saucepan and return to heat. Cook and stir until thickened; remove from heat. Allow to cool 10 minutes. Add sugar replacement, vanilla and melted margarine, and stir just to blend. Pour into 8 serving dishes. Serve hot or chilled.

Yield: 8 servings
Exchange 1 serving: ⅓ full-fat milk
Calories 1 serving: 65

Rice Pudding

1 qt.	low-fat milk (2% milkfat)	1 L
1 c.	rice (uncooked)	250 mL
1 t.	vanilla extract	5 mL
2 T.	granulated sugar replacement	30 mL
2 T.	margarine	30 mL
½ t.	cinnamon	2 mL
¼ t.	nutmeg	1 mL

Combine all ingredients in well-greased baking dish. Bake at 325 °F (165 °C) for 2 hours, or until knife inserted in center comes out clean. Stir occasionally for the first hour.

Microwave: Cook on Low for 30 to 35 minutes, or until knife inserted in center comes out clean. Turn dish a quarter turn every 5 minutes. Stir occasionally the first 15 minutes.

Yield: 9 servings
Exchange 1 serving: 1 low-fat milk, ½ fruit
Calories 1 serving: 111

Tapioca Custard Pudding

½ c.	tapioca	125 mL
1 qt.	milk	1 L
3 T.	granulated sugar replacement	45 mL
dash	salt	dash
2	egg yolks (slightly beaten)	2
2 t.	vanilla extract	10 mL

Combine tapioca, milk, sugar replacement and salt in medium sauce-pan; stir to blend. Allow to rest 10 minutes. Place pan on heat and bring to a boil. Reduce heat, and cook and stir until mixture thickens. Remove from heat. Pour small amount of hot tapioca mixture into egg yolks, stirring to blend. Pour egg yolk mixture back into the pan, and return to heat. Cook and stir until mixture thickens, or about 3 minutes. Remove from heat, stir in vanilla, and serve hot or cold.

Yield: 8 servings
Exchange 1 serving: 1 bread, 1 fat
Calories 1 serving: 110

Lo-Cal Chocolate Pudding

⅓ c.	cocoa	90 mL
¼ c.	granulated sugar replacement	60 mL
2 T.	cornstarch	30 mL
¼ t.	salt	1 mL
2 c.	skim milk	500 mL
1	egg (beaten)	1
1 T.	margarine	15 mL
1 t.	vanilla extract	5 mL

Combine cocoa, sugar replacement, cornstarch and salt in saucepan; stir in milk. Cook and stir over medium heat until thick and bubbly. Reduce heat; cook and stir 4 minutes more. Remove from heat. Stir small amount of hot cocoa mixture into beaten egg; pour egg mixture back into cocoa mixture. Stir to blend. Return saucepan to heat; cook 2 minutes more. Remove from heat; add margarine and vanilla.

Yield: 4 servings
Exchange 1 serving: 1 low-fat milk
Calories 1 serving: 107

Baked Plum Pudding

2	eggs	2
1	egg white	1
3 T.	granulated sugar replacement	45 mL
¼ c.	liquid shortening	60 mL
1 c.	unsweetened plum puree (baby food)	250 mL
1 c.	flour	250 mL
1 t.	baking soda	5 mL
½ t.	cinnamon	2 mL
¼ t.	nutmeg	1 mL
3 T.	skim milk	45 mL
2 T.	lemon juice	30 mL

Beat eggs and egg white until soft and fluffy; beat in sugar replacement, shortening and plum puree. Combine flour, baking soda, cinnamon and nutmeg in sifter. Combine milk and lemon juice in cup. Sift flour mixture alternately with milk mixture into plum mixture. Fold gently to mix completely. Pour into well-greased 9-in. (23-cm) square baking dish. Bake at 350 °F (175 °C) for 20 to 30 minutes, or until firm.

Yield: 9 servings
Exchange 1 serving: 1 bread
                          1 fat
Calories 1 serving: 144

Apricot Pudding

⅓ c.	unsweetened apricot puree (baby food)	90 mL
1 t.	baking soda	5 mL
1	egg (beaten)	1
½ c.	milk	125 mL
1 t.	lemon juice	5 mL
½ t.	almond extract	2 mL
1 T.	margarine (melted)	15 mL
1 c.	flour (sifted)	250 mL
2 T.	granulated sugar replacement	30 mL
dash	salt	dash

Combine apricot puree and baking soda in small mixing bowl; allow to rest 5 minutes. Combine remaining ingredients in large mixing bowl, add puree, and beat well to blend. Pour into well-greased 8-in. (20-cm) square baking dish, and bake at 350 °F (175 °C) for 1 hour. Allow to cool slightly before serving.

Yield: 8 servings
Exchange 1 serving: 1 bread
½ fat
Calories 1 serving: 90

Rhubarb Sponge Pudding

2 T.	margarine	30 mL
2 T.	granulated brown sugar replacement	30 mL
1 qt.	rhubarb, cut into 1-in. (2.5-cm) pieces	1 L
2	egg yolks	2
2 T.	granulated sugar replacement	30 mL
1 c.	flour	250 mL
½ t.	salt	2 mL
½ t.	baking powder	2 mL
½ c.	water	125 mL
1 t.	vanilla extract	5 mL
2	egg whites (stiffly beaten)	2

Melt margarine in small saucepan, add brown sugar replacement, and stir to blend. Spread mixture into bottom of 13 × 9-in. (33 × 23-cm) baking dish, and place rhubarb pieces evenly over the margarine mixture. Combine egg yolks and sugar replacement, beating until light and fluffy. Combine flour, salt and baking powder in sifter; beat alternately with water and vanilla into egg yolks. Fold egg yolk mixture completely into stiffly beaten egg whites and pour batter over rhubarb, spreading it out evenly. Bake at 350 °F (190 °C) for 45 minutes. Turn upside down on serving plate, and serve warm or cold.

Yield: 12 servings
Exchange 1 serving: ½ bread
½ fat
Calories 1 serving: 69

Indian Pudding

¼ c.	yellow cornmeal	60 mL
3 c.	skim milk	750 mL
¼ c.	molasses	60 mL
3 T.	margarine	45 mL
1	egg (slightly beaten)	1
2 T.	brown sugar replacement	30 mL
½ t.	cinnamon	2 mL
½ t.	nutmeg	2 mL
¼ t.	ginger	1 mL
¼ t.	salt	1 mL

Combine cornmeal and 1 c. (250 mL) of the milk in small bowl; allow to rest 15 minutes. Heat remaining milk in saucepan until warm (*do not boil*). Remove from heat and add cornmeal mixture and remaining ingredients. Pour into well-greased 1 qt. (1 L) baking dish and bake at 350 °F (175 °C) for 1½ hours, or until knife inserted in center comes out clean.

Microwave: Cook on Low for 25 minutes, or until knife inserted in center comes out clean. Turn dish a quarter turn every 5 minutes.

Yield: 8 servings
Exchange 1 serving: 1 bread
1 fat
Calories 1 serving: 120

Hasty Pudding

CAKE:

2 T.	margarine	30 mL
2 t.	granulated brown sugar replacement	10 mL
1 c.	flour (sifted)	250 mL
1½ t.	baking powder	7 mL
¼ t.	salt	1 mL
½ c.	skim milk	125 mL
½ c.	raisins	125 mL

Cream together margarine and sugar replacement. Combine flour, baking powder and salt, and add alternately with milk to creamed mixture. Fold in raisins. Pour batter into well-greased 8-in. (20-cm) baking dish.

SYRUP:

1 T.	flour		15 mL
2 c.	cold water		500 mL
2 T.	granulated brown sugar replacement		30 mL
2 t.	margarine		10 mL
1 t.	vanilla extract		5 mL

Combine flour and water in saucepan; cook and stir over medium heat until slightly thickened. Remove from heat. Add sugar replacement, margarine and vanilla, stirring to mix. Pour over cake batter, and bake at 350 °F (175 °C) for 45 minutes.

Yield: 9 servings
Exchange 1 serving: 1 bread
1 fruit
1 fat
Calories 1 serving: 84

Baked Custard

2½ c.	low-fat milk (2% milkfat)	625 mL
3 T.	granulated sugar replacement	45 mL
¼ t.	salt	1 mL
1 t.	vanilla extract	5 mL
3	eggs	3
	nutmeg	

Combine milk, sugar replacement, salt, vanilla and eggs in large bowl; beat to blend well. Pour into six ½-c. (125-mL) individual baking cups; sprinkle with nutmeg. Set cups in large baking pan. Add 1 in. (2.5 cm) of water to pan; bake custard at 350 °F (175 °C) for 45 minutes, or until knife inserted in center comes out clean.

Microwave: Cook on Defrost for 15 to 17 minutes. Turn dish a quarter turn every 5 minutes. Allow to set 5 minutes before serving.

Yield: 6 servings
Exchange 1 serving: ½ fruit
½ medium-fat meat
Calories 1 serving: 82

Caramel Custard Cup

1 T.	lo-cal maple syrup	15 mL
1	egg	1
½ c.	evaporated skimmed milk	125 mL
⅓ c.	water	90 mL
1 T.	granulated sugar replacement	15 mL
1 t.	vanilla extract	5 mL
dash	salt	dash

Divide maple syrup evenly between 2 custard cups. Combine egg, milk, water, sugar replacement, vanilla and salt in mixing bowl; beat or whisk until well blended. Carefully pour custard mixture over syrup in custard cups. Set cups in shallow pan holding 1 in. (2.5 cm) of water. Bake at 350 °F (175 °C) for 50 minutes, or until knife inserted in center comes out clean.

Microwave: *Water bath not needed.* Cook on Low for 8 to 10 minutes, or until edges are set and center is soft but not runny. Allow to rest 10 to 15 minutes before serving.

Yield: 2 servings
Exchange 1 serving: 1 lean meat
½ fruit
Calories 1 serving: 85

Creamy Chocolate Mousse

⅓ c.	cocoa	90 mL
1 t.	instant coffee	5 mL
¼ c.	granulated sugar replacement	60 mL
2 T.	cornstarch	30 mL
¼ t.	salt	1 mL
2 c.	skim milk	500 mL
1	egg (beaten)	1
8-oz. pkg.	cream cheese (softened)	240-g pkg.
1 t.	vanilla	5 mL

Combine cocoa, coffee, sugar replacement, cornstarch and salt in saucepan; stir in milk. Cook and stir over medium heat until thick and bubbly, reduce heat, and then cook and stir 4 minutes more. Remove from heat. Stir small amount of hot mixture into beaten egg and pour egg mixture into hot mixture, stirring to blend. Cook over low heat for 2 minutes and remove from heat. Add cream cheese and vanilla, beating until well blended and fluffy. Pour into 1 qt. (1 L) mould or dish, cover with waxed paper and chill until firm. Remove paper and unmould.

Yield: 10 servings
Exchange 1 serving: 1 full-fat milk
                          1 fat
Calories 1 serving: 128

Marshmallow Crème

3 env.	unflavored gelatin	3 env.
¼ c.	cold water	60 mL
¾ c.	boiling water	190 mL
3 T.	granulated sugar replacement	45 mL
	or granulated fructose	
1 t.	white vanilla extract	5 mL
3	egg whites	3

Sprinkle gelatin over cold water in mixing bowl; set aside 5 minutes to soften. Add to boiling water in saucepan, cook and stir until gelatin is dissolved. Remove from heat. Cool to consistency of thick syrup. Add sugar replacement and vanilla, stirring to blend. Beat egg whites into soft peaks. Very slowly, trickle a small stream of gelatin mixture into egg whites, beating until all gelatin mixture is blended. Continue beating until light and fluffy. Pour into prepared pan.

FOR MARSHMALLOWS: Fill 13 × 9 × 2-in. (33 × 23 × 5-cm) pan with flour or cornstarch to desired depth. Form moulds with small glass, inside of dough cutter or object of desired size by pressing form into flour to the bottom of the pan. Spoon marshmallow crème into mould and refrigerate until set. Dust or roll tops in flour; shake off excess. Keep refrigerated.

Optional marshmallows: Lightly grease and flour 13 × 9-in. (33 × 23-cm) baking dish. Pour marshmallow crème in dish, spreading out evenly. Refrigerate until set and cut to desired size.

Yield: 4 c. (1000 mL)
Exchange 1 c. (250 mL): Negligible
Calories 1 c. (250 mL): 11

Coffee Crème

1	egg	1
2 t.	granulated sugar replacement	10 mL
⅓ c.	milk	90 mL
¼ c.	strong coffee	60 mL

Beat egg and sugar replacement until light and fluffy. Combine milk and coffee and heat just to boiling. Blend milk mixture into egg mixture, and pour into well-greased individual baking cup. Place cup in shallow pan; add water to pan until about halfway up the cup. Bake at 325 °F (165 °C) for 15 minutes, or until done.

Microwave: Place cup in microwave oven. Cook on Defrost for 5 to 7 minutes, or until done.

Yield: 1 serving
Exchange: 1 medium-fat meat
　　　　　⅓ milk
Calories: 124

Crème de Menthe

1 c.	Marshmallow Crème (p. 71)	250 mL
6 drops	green peppermint flavoring	6 drops
2 T.	water	30 mL
1 env.	lo-cal whipped topping mix (prepared)	1 env.

Combine marshmallow crème, flavoring and water in saucepan. Cook and fold gently over low heat until marshmallow crème is slightly melted. Remove from heat; cool. Fold into topping and pour into freezer tray. Freeze until firm but not solid. Scrape into mixing bowl, beating to loosen, and spoon into 8 individual serving dishes.

Yield: 8 servings
Exchange 1 serving: ⅓ fat
Calories 1 serving: 16

Whipped Banana Yogurt

½ c.	fresh or frozen (reconstituted) orange juice	125 mL
	peel of 1 orange (grated)	
4	bananas, cut into 1-in. (2.5-cm) pieces	4
2 t.	fresh lemon juice	10 mL
1 c.	plain low-fat yogurt	250 mL
2	egg whites	2

Combine orange juice and orange peel in small saucepan; cook and stir over medium heat until peel is tender. Let cool; refrigerate. Combine banana pieces and lemon juice in mixing bowl or food processor. Whip to puree; add orange juice and mix together. Add yogurt and whip just to blend. Pour into 8-in. (20-cm) round cake pan and freeze until firm.

Remove from freezer and let mixture soften slightly, just until it can easily be spooned out of pan. Place in mixing bowl or food processor; mix until smooth and fluffy. With machine running, add egg whites and mix thoroughly. Return to cake pan and freeze. Remove from freezer and allow to soften slightly. Turn into mixing bowl or food processor and whip until soft, light and smooth. Spoon into individual dishes and serve immediately.

Yield: 8 servings
Exchange 1 serving: 1 bread
Calories 1 serving: 73

ICE CREAM, ICES AND FROZEN DESSERTS

Ice Cream Cones

2T.	margarine (melted)	30 mL
2T.	granulated brown sugar replacement	30 mL
1 T.	granulated sugar replacement	15 mL
1	egg	1
1 t.	vanilla extract	5 mL
1¼ c.	flour	310 mL
1¼ c.	water	310 mL

Combine all ingredients in blender, food processor or mixing bowl. Beat until smooth.

FOR CREPE PAN: Pour batter into 9-in. (23-cm) pie tin. Heat crepe pan until hot, and dip crepe pan into batter. Fry batter until edges are lightly browned. With spatula, turn crepe over. Press lightly to help conform to pan. Fry until completely dry. Using spatula and cone, quickly roll batter into shape. Dry and cool on rack.

FOR KRUMKAKE IRON: Heat iron and place 1 T. (15 mL) mixture in center. Fry on both sides. Using spatula and cone, quickly roll batter into shape. Dry and cool on rack.

Yield: 36 cones
Exchange 1 cone: ¼ fruit
Calories 1 cone: 20

French Vanilla Ice Cream

5	egg yolks	5
¼ c.	granulated sugar replacement	60 mL
dash	salt	dash
2 c.	evaporated skimmed milk	500 mL
1-in. piece	vanilla bean	2.5-cm piece
2 c.	lo-cal whipped topping (prepared)	500 mL

Combine egg yolks, sugar replacement and salt in top of double boiler. Beat until frothy. Beat in milk and add vanilla bean. Cook and stir over simmering water until mixture is thick and vanilla bean is dissolved. Cool completely. With electric beater, beat well, and then fold in topping. Pour into freezer trays, cover with waxed paper, and freeze for 1 hour. Scrape into large bowl and beat until smooth and fluffy. Return to freezer trays. Cover. Freeze firm.

Yield: 1½ qt. (1½ L)
Exchange ½ c. (125 mL): ½ high-fat meat
Calories ½ c. (125 mL): 61

Vanilla Ice Cream Variations

CHOCOLATE:
Substitute ¼ c. (60 mL) cocoa and 2 T. (30 mL) granulated sugar replacement dissolved in 3 T. (45 mL) strong coffee for vanilla bean.

Exchange ½ c. (125 mL): ½ high-fat meat
Calories ½ c. (125 mL): 63

MAPLE:
Substitute granulated brown sugar replacement for sugar replacement and 1 T. maple flavor for vanilla bean.

Exchange ½ c. (125 mL): ½ high-fat meat
Calories ½ c. (125 mL): 61

PECAN:
Fold in ½ c. (125 mL) finely ground pecans after final beating.

Exchange ½ c. (125 mL): ½ high-fat meat
                          ½ fat
Calories ½ c. (125 mL): 91

Strawberry Ice Cream

1 qt.	evaporated skimmed milk	1 L
2	eggs	2
3 T.	granulated sugar replacement	45 mL
¼ t.	salt	1 mL
¼ c.	lemon juice	60 mL
2 c.	strawberries (sliced)	500 mL
2 drops	red food color	2 drops

Chill milk. Beat eggs until frothy. Add sugar replacement, salt and lemon juice to the eggs, and beat well. Gradually beat in the cold milk.

For ice cream freezer: Pour mixture into 1-gal. (4-L) freezer can. Freeze as directed by manufacturer. Add strawberries and food color when cream begins to thicken.

For tray freezing: Pour into 3 freezer trays, and freeze until crystals form on edge of trays. Pour into large bowl; beat well. Add strawberries and food color, and return to trays. Repeat for lighter ice cream. Repack in ice cream or plastic cartons; freeze until firm.

Yield: 8 servings
Exchange 1 serving: 1 nonfat milk
⅓ fat
Calories 1 serving: 104

Quick Orange Ice Cream

½ c.	orange juice concentrate (thawed)	125 mL
1 env.	lo-cal whipped topping mix	1 env.
½ t.	lemon juice	2 mL

Combine all ingredients in a small narrow bowl. Whip at high speed until thick and fluffy. Pour into freezer tray and freeze until firm.

Yield: 6 servings
Exchange per serving: 1 fruit
1 fat
Calories per serving: 83

Pineapple-Orange Ice Cream

2	eggs	2
3 T.	granulated sugar replacement	45 mL
¼ t.	salt	1 mL
1 qt.	evaporated skimmed milk (cold)	1 L
2 c.	unsweetened crushed pineapple (with juice)	500 mL
1 c.	orange juice	250 mL
2 T.	orange rind (grated)	30 mL

Beat eggs until frothy. Add sugar replacement and salt; beat well. Gradually beat in milk. Stir in pineapple, orange juice and rind.

For ice cream freezer: Pour into 1-gal. (4-L) freezer can. Freeze as directed by manufacturer.

For tray freezing: Pour into 3 freezer trays. Freeze until mushy. Pour into large bowl; beat well. Return to freezer trays. Repeat. Repack in ice cream or plastic cartons. Freeze firm.

Yield: 1 gal. (4 L)
Exchange ½ c. (125 mL): ⅕ bread
Calories ½ c. (125 mL): 22

Date Parfait

½ c.	dates (chopped)	125 mL
1½ c.	water	375 mL
4	egg yolks (well beaten)	4
½ c.	orange juice	125 mL
1 c.	lo-cal whipped topping (prepared)	250 mL

Combine dates and water in saucepan. Cook and stir occasionally over medium heat for 25 minutes; let cool. Add beaten egg yolks and orange juice; cook and stir constantly over low heat until thickened. Chill. Fold topping into date mixture, spread evenly into freezer tray, and freeze until firm.

Yield: 8 servings
Exchange 1 serving: 1 fruit
                        ½ fat
Calories 1 serving: 55

Mint-Chip Ice Cream

1½ t.	unflavored gelatin	7 mL
2 T.	boiling water	30 mL
2 t.	green peppermint flavoring	10 mL
¼ t.	salt	1 mL
1 env.	lo-cal whipped topping mix	1 env.
½ c.	cold water	125 mL
1 t.	vanilla extract	5 mL
¼ c.	small semisweet chocolate chips	60 mL

Sprinkle gelatin over boiling water, stirring to dissolve. Add peppermint flavoring and salt; stir well. Let mixture cool. Combine topping mix, cold water and vanilla in bowl, and whip mixture until stiff. Fold in peppermint mixture and chocolate chips. Pour into freezer tray and freeze until firm.

Yield: 6 servings
Exchange 1 serving: ½ fruit
2 fat
Calories 1 serving: 78

Heavenly Hash

⅓ c.	Marshmallow Crème (p. 71)	90 mL
1 c.	skim milk	250 mL
1 c.	almonds (chopped)	250 mL
½ c.	walnuts (chopped)	125 mL
1 c.	Bing cherries (pitted)	250 mL
1 c.	lo-cal whipped topping (prepared)	250 mL

Dissolve Marshmallow Crème in milk over hot water; cool. Add nuts and cherries and fold in topping. Pour mixture into freezer tray; freeze until mushy. Scrape into a bowl and stir vigorously. Return to freezer tray and freeze firm.

Yield: 8 servings
Exchange 1 serving: ⅔ full-fat milk
1 fat
Calories 1 serving: 179

Raisin Ice Cream Sandwich

½ c.	raisins	125 mL
½ c.	water	125 mL
1½ c.	flour	375 mL
1 t.	baking soda	5 mL
¼ t.	salt	1 mL
¼ c.	solid shortening (soft)	60 mL
3 T.	granulated sugar replacement	45 mL
1	egg	1
⅔ c.	buttermilk	160 mL
2 c.	ice milk (softened)	500 mL

Combine raisins and water in saucepan. Bring to a boil, reduce heat and simmer 5 minutes. Remove from heat; allow to cool slightly. Drain. Combine flour, baking soda and salt in sifter, and sift twice. Return flour mixture to sifter. Cream together shortening and sugar replacement in medium mixing bowl. Add egg and beat well. Add sifted-flour mixture alternately with buttermilk, beating well after each addition. Stir in drained raisins. Pour mixture into a well-greased and floured 9-in. (23-cm) square pan. Bake at 350 °F (175 °C) for 30 to 40 minutes, or until done. Cut into 9 squares. Cut horizontally through center of each square and fill evenly with softened ice milk. Freeze until firm.

Yield: 9 servings
Exchange 1 serving: 2 bread
                       1½ fat
Calories 1 serving: 205

Kid's Quick Ice

¼ c.	granulated sugar replacement	60 mL
1 env.	unsweetened fruit drink mix	1 env.
3 c.	crushed ice	750 mL

Combine all ingredients in blender or food processor. Beat just until blended. Scoop into cups; eat as is or freeze.

Yield: 2 c. (500 mL)
Exchange: Negligible
Calories: Negligible

Apricot Ice

¼ c.	granulated sugar replacement	60 mL
1 c.	water	250 mL
1 t.	cornstarch	5 mL
1 c.	unsweetened apricot puree	250 mL
2 T.	lemon juice	30 mL

Combine sugar replacement, water and cornstarch in saucepan; bring to a boil. Reduce heat and simmer 5 minutes. Add apricot puree and lemon juice. Pour into freezer tray and cover with waxed paper. Freeze until firm.

For fluffy ice: Freeze until mushy. Scrape into mixing bowl or blender and beat just until loosened. Return to freezer tray.

Yield: 6 servings
Exchange 1 serving: 1 fruit
Calories 1 serving: 40

Strawberry Ice

¼ c.	granulated sugar replacement	60 mL
1 c.	water	250 mL
1 t.	cornstarch	5 mL
1 c.	strawberries (pureed)	250 mL
1 T.	lemon juice	15 mL
	red food color	

Combine sugar replacement, water and cornstarch in saucepan; bring to a boil. Reduce heat and simmer 5 minutes. Stir in strawberry puree, lemon juice and a few drops of red food color. Pour into freezer tray and cover with waxed paper. Freeze until firm.

For fluffy ice: Freeze until mushy. Scrape into mixing bowl or blender and beat just until loosened. Return to freezer tray.

Yield: 4 servings
Exchange 1 serving: ⅓ fruit
Calories 1 serving: 14

Citrus Ice

¼ c.	granulated sugar replacement	60 mL
1 c.	water	250 mL
1 env.	unflavored gelatin	1 env.
1 c.	unsweetened grapefruit juice	250 mL
1 c.	unsweetened orange juice	250 mL
¼ c.	lemon juice	60 mL

Combine sugar replacement, water and gelatin in saucepan; bring to a boil. Reduce heat and simmer 5 minutes. Cool slightly. Stir in juices and freeze.

For fluffy ice: Freeze until mushy. Scrape into mixing bowl or blender and beat just until loosened. Return to freezer tray.

Yield: 5 servings
Exchange 1 serving: 1 fruit
Calories 1 serving: 41

Cranberry Sherbet

2 c.	fresh cranberries	500 mL
1½ c.	boiling water	375 mL
¼ c.	orange juice	60 mL
1 T.	orange rind	30 mL
½ t.	salt	2 mL
2 t.	unflavored gelatin	30 mL
½ c.	granulated sugar replacement	125 mL

Cook cranberries in the boiling water until soft and skins have popped. Pour into blender. Add orange juice, rind and salt, and blend to puree. Combine with gelatin, bring to a boil, and cook for 3 to 5 minutes. Remove from heat. Add sugar replacement and stir to dissolve; cool. Pour into 2 freezer trays and freeze until almost firm. Scrape into mixing bowl and beat until light and fluffy. Return to trays and refreeze.

Yield: 12 servings
Exchange: Negligible
Calories: Negligible

Lemon Sherbet

6-oz. can	frozen lemonade concentrate	170-g can
3 T.	granulated sugar replacement	45 mL
	or granulated fructose	
¼ t.	salt	1 mL
2 T.	lemon rind	30 mL
3 c.	evaporated skimmed milk (cold)	750 mL

Combine all ingredients in large bowl; beat well.

For ice cream freezer: Pour into 1-gal. (4-L) freezer can. Freeze as directed by manufacturer.

For tray freezing: Pour into 2 freezer trays and freeze until mushy. Pour into large bowl; beat well. Repack in trays or plastic cartons and freeze until firm.

Yield: ½ gal. (2 L)
Exchange ½ c. (125 mL) with sugar replacement: 1 fruit
Calories ½ c. (125 mL) with sugar replacement: 43
Exchange ½ c. (125 mL) with fructose: 1 fruit
Calories ½ c. (125 mL) with fructose: 51

Strawberry Mallowbet

1 c.	Marshmallow Crème (p. 71)	250 mL
2 c.	skim milk	500 mL
1½ c.	fresh strawberries (slightly crushed)	375 mL
2 T.	lemon juice	30 mL

Combine Marshmallow Crème and 2 T. (30 mL) of the milk in saucepan. Cook and gently fold until crème is slightly melted. Remove from heat. Continue folding until mixture is smooth and spongy; let cool. Blend remaining milk, crushed strawberries and lemon juice into marshmallow mixture. Pour into freezer tray and freeze until firm. Stir occasionally.

Yield: 8 servings
Exchange 1 serving: ½ fruit
Calories 1 serving: 32

Cola Sherbet

1 c.	Marshmallow Crème (p. 71)	250 mL
2 c.	diet cola	500 mL
dash	salt	dash
2 T.	lemon juice	30 mL

Combine all ingredients. Beat until smooth and fluffy. Pour into freezer tray and freeze until firm. Stir 2 or 3 times while freezing.

Yield: 6 servings
Exchange 1 serving: Negligible
Calories 1 serving: Negligible

Pineapple Mallowbet

1 c.	unsweetened crushed pineapple (with juice)	250 mL
1 c.	Marshmallow Crème (p. 71)	250 mL
1 env.	lo-cal whipped topping mix (prepared)	1 env.

Drain pineapple juice into saucepan; reserve pineapple. Add Marshmallow Crème to pineapple juice. Cook and gently fold over low heat until crème is slightly melted and then remove from heat. Continue folding until mixture is smooth and spongy; let cool. Fold in pineapple, then the topping. Pour into freezer tray; freeze till firm.

Yield: 8 servings
Exchange 1 serving: ⅓ fruit, ⅓ fat
Calories 1 serving: 26

Orange Freeze

3 c.	crushed ice	750 mL
1 pkg.	lo-cal orange drink mix	1 pkg.
½ c.	granulated sugar replacement	125 mL

Combine all ingredients in blender. Whip on high speed.

Yield: 4 servings
Exchange: Negligible
Calories: Negligible

Chocolate Banana Mousse

1-oz. sq.	unsweetened chocolate	28-g sq.
1 c.	evaporated skimmed milk	250 mL
3 T.	granulated sugar replacement	45 mL
2	egg yolks	2
¼ t.	salt	1 mL
1 t.	vanilla extract	5 mL
2	bananas (sliced)	2

Combine chocolate, ¼ c. (60 mL) of the milk and the sugar replacement in top of double boiler. (Chill remaining milk in freezer.) Cook and stir over simmering water until chocolate melts. Pour small amount of hot chocolate mixture over egg yolks and beat well. Pour egg mixture into chocolate mixture in top of double boiler. Stir in salt. Cook and stir over hot water until mixture thickens. Cool completely. Scrape cold or slightly frozen milk into mixing bowl and beat until very stiff. Fold chocolate mixture into stiffly beaten milk. Fold in vanilla and banana slices. Spoon into mould, freezer tray or individual cups and freeze until firm.

Yield: 8 servings
Exchange 1 serving: 1 bread, ½ fat
Calories 1 serving: 69

Cranberry Mousse

1 c.	cranberries	250 mL
1 c.	water	250 mL
½ c.	orange juice	125 mL
1 T.	liquid sugar replacement	15 mL
2 c.	lo-cal whipped topping (prepared)	500 mL

Combine cranberries and water in saucepan. Cook and stir until cranberries are popped, soft and thickened. Remove from heat; cool slightly. Stir in orange juice and sugar replacement; cool completely. Fold topping into cranberry mixture. Spoon into mould, freezer trays or individual cups, and freeze until firm.

Yield: 8 servings
Exchange 1 serving: 1 fat
Calories 1 serving: 36

Pecan Mousse

½ c.	pecans (chopped)	125 mL
1 t.	unflavored gelatin	5 mL
2 T.	cold water	30 mL
1½ c.	evaporated skimmed milk	375 mL
1 T.	liquid sugar replacement	15 mL
	or	
2 T.	granulated fructose	30 mL
1 T.	vanilla extract	15 mL

Brown pecans in cake pan in 350 °F (175 °C) oven (about 10 minutes). Shake occasionally. Sprinkle gelatin over cold water and allow to rest 5 minutes to soften. Combine milk and soften gelatin in saucepan; cook and stir over medium heat until gelatin is dissolved. Remove from heat. Add browned pecans, liquid sugar replacement and vanilla. Stir to blend well. Pour into mould, freezer tray or individual dishes and freeze until firm.

Yield: 8 servings
Exchange 1 serving with sugar replacement: ½ full-fat milk
Calories 1 serving with sugar replacement: 72
Exchange 1 serving with fructose: ½ full-fat milk
Calories 1 serving with fructose: 85

Watermelon Granite

2 c.	watermelon (without seeds)	500 mL
1 T.	lemon juice	15 mL
2 T.	granulated sugar replacement	30 mL

Combine all ingredients in blender or food processor and beat to puree. Pour into freezer tray and freeze until firm but not hard. Scrape back into blender or food processor, beating to sherbet consistency. Cantaloupe or honeydew melon may be substituted for the watermelon.

Yield: 1 c. (250 mL)
Exchange: Negligible
Calories: Negligible

Pistachio Frozen Dessert

¼	Sponge Cake (p. 124)	¼
1 c.	lo-cal whipped topping (prepared)	250 mL
2 T.	granulated sugar replacement	30 mL
	or granulated fructose	
¼ c.	pistachio nuts (chopped)	60 mL
1 t.	almond extract	5 mL
	green food color	
1	egg white	1
dash	salt	dash

Thinly slice the sponge cake. Line bottom and sides of mould or freezer tray with two-thirds of the slices. Reserve remaining slices for top. Combine topping, sugar replacement, nuts, almond extract and a few drops of food color in mixing bowl. Beat or stir to blend. Refrigerate. Combine egg white and salt in narrow mixing bowl and beat until very stiff. Fold egg white into whipped-topping mixture. Spread evenly over sponge cake in mould. Cover with remaining slices of sponge cake, and freeze until firm. Unmould.

Yield: 6 servings
Exchange 1 serving with sugar replacement: ½ full-fat milk
Calories 1 serving with sugar replacement: 93
Exchange 1 serving with fructose: ½ full-fat milk
⅓ fruit
Calories 1 serving with fructose: 105

FRUIT DESSERTS AND TOPPINGS

Spiced Purple Plums

4	purple plums (firm)	4
½ c.	water	125 mL
1 whole	clove	1 whole
1	bay leaf	1
1 stick	cinnamon	1 stick
1 T.	granulated sugar replacement	15 mL

Peel, pit and quarter plums. Combine water, clove, bay leaf, cinnamon and sugar replacement in saucepan. Bring just to boiling; add plums. Bring back to boiling, reduce heat and cook 5 minutes. With a slotted spoon, remove plums to heated serving dish.

Yield: 2 servings
Exchange 1 serving: 1 fruit
Calories 1 serving: 51

Poached Figs

1 c.	water	250 mL
¼ c.	wine vinegar	60 mL
3 T.	granulated sugar replacement	45 mL
2	cinnamon sticks	2
15	dried figs	15

Combine water, vinegar, sugar replacement and cinnamon sticks in saucepan, and bring to a boil. Add figs, reduce heat, cover, and simmer for 15 minutes. Add extra water if needed. Remove figs with slotted spoon. Chill thoroughly.

Yield: 15 servings
Exchange 1 serving: 1 fruit
Calories 1 serving: 60

Strawberries Romanoff

2 c.	fresh strawberries (hulled)	500 mL
1 c.	French Vanilla Ice Cream (softened), p. 75	250 mL
1 T.	Orange Marmalade (p. 90)	15 mL
2 t.	rum extract	10 mL
½ c.	lo-cal whipped topping (prepared)	125 mL

Divide strawberries evenly between 4 serving dishes and chill thoroughly. At serving time, fold together ice cream, orange marmalade, rum extract and topping. Spoon over cold strawberries. Serve immediately.

Yield: 4 servings
Exchange 1 serving: ½ fruit
        ½ medium-fat meat
        1 fat
Calories 1 serving: 75

Berries with Crème

1½ c.	creamed cottage cheese	375 mL
¼ c.	buttermilk	60 mL
2 c.	fresh blueberries (rinsed)	500 mL
2 c.	fresh raspberries (rinsed)	500 mL

Place cottage cheese in strainer over bowl. Drain thoroughly for at least 1 hour in refrigerator. Add buttermilk to cottage cheese liquid; stir to blend. Cover and refrigerate dry cottage cheese mixture. Gently combine blueberries with half of milk mixture, and the raspberries with the remaining half. Cover both and refrigerate. Shortly before serving, mould one-sixth of the cottage cheese into the center of each of the 6 chilled dessert plates. Arrange one-sixth of the blueberries opposite one-sixth of the raspberries in a crescent pattern around each mound of cottage cheese. Serve immediately.

Yield: 6 servings
Exchange 1 serving: 1 fruit
        1 lean meat
Calories 1 serving: 94

Fruit Flower

¼ c.	buttermilk	60 mL
2 t.	granulated sugar replacement	10 mL
2 t.	cornstarch	10 mL
3 T.	hazelnuts (skinned)	45 mL
1	peach (firm)	1
1	purple plum (firm)	1
1	red plum (firm)	1
	lemon juice	
6	sour cherries	6

Combine buttermilk, sugar replacement and cornstarch in small saucepan. Cook and stir over low heat until thickened. Toast hazelnuts and process them in blender or food processor until they are fine crumbs; reserve.

Peel, pit and slice peach and plums. Dip in lemon juice. Pit cherries. Arrange sliced fruit alternately in circle on two small serving plates. Spoon thickened milk in center and top with cherries. Sprinkle toasted hazelnut crumbs over fruit plate. Serve immediately.

Yield: 2 servings
Exchange 1 serving: 1 bread
　　　　　　　　　　1 fat
Calories 1 serving: 124

Christmas Pear

1	pear	1
½ c.	water	125 mL
2 T.	granulated sugar replacement	30 mL
4 drops	red food color	4 drops
1-in. stick	cinnamon	2.5-cm stick

Peel and core pear. Cut in half or into slices. Combine water, sugar replacement, food color and cinnamon stick in saucepan. Bring to a boil, add the pear, reduce heat and simmer for 3 minutes. Turn pear several times to completely color. Remove with slotted spoon. Serve hot or cold.

Yield: 1 serving
Exchange: 1 fruit
Calories: 60

Apricot-Banana Sauté

4	apricots	4
1	banana	1
2 t.	margarine	10 mL
1 T.	lo-cal maple syrup	15 mL
1 t.	almond extract	5 mL
½ t.	vanilla extract	2 mL

Peel, pit and quarter apricots. Peel and slice bananas into 1-in. (2.5-cm) slices. Melt margarine in skillet, add maple syrup and extracts, and stir just to blend. Add fruit and sauté, turning once, for 2 minutes. Spoon into heated serving dishes.

Yield: 2 servings
Exchange 1 serving: 2 fruit
⅓ bread
Calories 1 serving: 126

Orange Marmalade

1	orange	1
1 c.	water	250 mL
1 T.	lo-cal pectin	15 mL
1 t.	granulated sugar replacement	5 mL

With a vegetable peeler, remove peel from orange. Combine orange peel and water in saucepan, bring to boil, and boil for 3 minutes. Cut off membrane from fruit. Place fruit, orange water (with peel) and pectin in blender or food processor. Work until completely blended. Pour into saucepan, bring to boil, and boil for 1 minute. Allow to cool slightly. Stir in sugar replacement. Pour into serving dish or jelly jar. Chill.

Microwave: Follow directions using at least 1-qt. (1-L) microwave dish. Cook on High.

Yield: 1¼ c. (310 mL)
Exchange 2 T. (30 mL): ⅕ fruit
Calories 2 T. (30 mL): 10

Red Fruit Compote

1-lb. can	tart cherries	460-g can
10-oz. pkg.	unsweetened frozen raspberries (thawed)	280-g pkg.
10-oz. pkg.	unsweetened frozen strawberries (thawed)	280-g pkg.
2 T.	granulated sugar replacement	30 mL
2 T.	cornstarch	30 mL
1 T.	lemon juice	15 mL

Drain fruit; reserve liquids. Add enough water to reserved fruit liquid to make 2½ c. (625 mL). Blend liquid, sugar replacement and cornstarch in saucepan; cook and stir over medium heat until clear and thickened. Remove from heat; stir in lemon juice. Fold in cherries, raspberries and strawberries. Chill thoroughly.

Yield: 8 servings
Exchange 1 serving: 1 fruit
Calories 1 serving: 42

Frozen Fruit

¼ c.	fresh grapefruit sections	60 mL
¼ c.	fresh orange sections	60 mL
¼ c.	fresh tart cherries	60 mL
¼ c.	banana slices	60 mL
1 t.	lemon juice	5 mL
1 t.	unflavored gelatin	5 mL
2 T.	cold water	15 mL
1 t.	liquid sugar replacement	5 mL
1 c.	lo-cal whipped topping (prepared)	250 mL

Combine fruits and lemon juice in bowl; toss to coat. Cover and refrigerate. Sprinkle gelatin over cold water, and allow it to rest 5 minutes to soften. Heat just until gelatin is completely dissolved. Add gelatin and sugar replacement to fruit; toss to coat. Fold topping into fruit mixture. Spoon into mould, freezer tray or individual dishes. Freeze until firm.

Yield: 8 servings
Exchange 1 serving: ½ fruit
⅓ fat
Calories 1 serving: 29

Cranberry 'N' Peach

6	fresh peach halves, peeled	6
	lemon juice	
1¼ c.	unsweetened cranberry juice	310 mL
1 T.	cornstarch	15 mL
2 T.	granulated sugar replacement	30 mL
½ t.	orange peel (grated)	2 mL
¼ t.	salt	1 mL
1 stick	cinnamon	1 stick
5	whole cloves	5

Dip peach halves in lemon juice to preserve color; place in serving dish. Combine cranberry juice, cornstarch, sugar replacement, orange peel, salt, cinnamon stick and cloves in saucepan. Cook and stir over medium heat until mixture boils and is clear. Remove from heat. Remove cinnamon stick and cloves, and pour hot liquid over peaches. Serve hot or cold.

Yield: 6 servings
Exchange 1 serving: ½ fruit
Calories 1 serving: 22

Melon and Grapes

½	cantaloupe melon	½
1 c.	green grapes	250 mL
¼ c.	buttermilk	60 mL
1 t.	liquid sugar replacement	5 mL
1 t.	water	5 mL

Peel and cube melon into the size of the grapes and place in bowl. Peel grapes and add to melon. Combine buttermilk, sugar replacement and water in cup, stirring to blend. Pour over fruit mixture. Fold in gently to coat the fruit. Cover and refrigerate at least 1 hour. Drain thoroughly and divide between 2 cold serving dishes. Serve immediately.

Yield: 2 servings
Exchange 1 serving: 1 fruit
Calories 1 serving: 72

Apple Fritters

⅓ c.	flour	90 mL
½ t.	baking powder	2 mL
dash	salt	dash
2 T.	milk	30 mL
1	apple (peeled and sliced)	1

Combine flour, baking powder, salt and milk in small bowl, beating until smooth. If batter is too stiff, add a little water. Dip apple slices into batter and fry until golden brown.

Yield: 2 servings
Exchange 1 serving: 1 bread
Calories 1 serving: 105

Apple Dumplings

1 recipe	Basic Pie Shell (p. 114)	1 recipe
4	apples	4
1 T.	lemon juice	15 mL
3 T.	granulated sugar replacement or granulated fructose	45 mL
¼ t.	cinnamon	2 mL
4 t.	margarine	20 mL
1	egg white (slightly beaten)	1

Roll out pie dough and cut into 4 equal pieces. Peel and core apples and sprinkle them with lemon juice. Place 1 apple in center of each piece of dough. Combine sugar replacement and cinnamon in a bowl, sprinkling evenly into cavity of apples. Top each apple with 1 t. (5 mL) margarine. Bring opposite ends of dough up over apple. Moisten slightly with water; seal securely. Brush with beaten egg white and place in shallow baking pan. Bake at 425 °F (220 °C) for 35 to 45 minutes, or until pastry is golden brown.

Yield: 4 dumplings
Exchange 1 dumpling: 2 bread
  1 fruit
  2½ fat
Calories 1 dumpling: 221

Pure Juice Jellies or Toppings

1 c.	fruit juice (unsweetened)	250 mL
1 T.	granulated sugar replacement	15 mL
1 T.	lo-cal pectin	15 mL

Combine ingredients in saucepan and bring to a boil. Boil for 2 minutes, remove from heat, and let cool slightly. Pour mixture into serving dish or jelly jar; chill.

Microwave: Follow directions, using large bowl. Cook on High.

Yield: ⅔ c. (189 mL)

APPLE JUICE: **Exchange 1 T. (15 mL):** ⅓ fruit
Calories 1 T. (15 mL): 10

CRANBERRY JUICE (unsweetened): **Exchange:** Negligible
Calories: Negligible

GRAPEFRUIT JUICE: **Exchange 1 T. (15 mL):** ⅕ fruit
Calories 1 T. (15 mL): 8

GRAPE JUICE: **Exchange 1. T. (15 mL):** ⅓ fruit
Calories 1 T. (15 mL): 13

PINEAPPLE JUICE: **Exchange 1 T. (15 mL):** ⅓ fruit
Calories 1 T. (15 mL): 9

Plum Whip

½ lb.	fresh plums	250 g
1 t.	lemon juice	5 mL
1	egg white	1
1 T.	granulated sugar replacement	15 mL

Pit and quarter plums. Puree plums and lemon juice in blender or food processor. Beat egg white and sugar replacement into stiff peaks. Gradually, beat plum puree into egg-white mixture. Spoon into dessert glasses.

Yield: 4 servings
Exchange 1 serving: 1 fruit
Calories 1 serving: 38

Strawberry Preserves or Topping

1 c.	fresh or frozen strawberries (unsweetened)	250 mL
1 t.	lo-cal pectin	5 mL
1 t.	granulated sugar replacement	5 mL

Place strawberries in top of double boiler, and mash slightly. Cook over boiling water until soft and juicy, crushing berries against sides of double boiler. Add pectin and sugar replacement, blending thoroughly. Cook until medium thick. Remove from heat and allow to cool slightly. Pour preserves into a jar or bowl. Preserves can also be made with blueberries or raspberries.

Microwave: Place strawberries in glass bowl; cover. Cook on High for 4 minutes, or until soft and juicy, crushing berries against sides of bowl. Add pectin and sugar replacement; blend in thoroughly. Cook on High for 30 seconds.

Yield: ⅔ c. (180 mL)
Exchange 2 T. (30 mL): ⅕ fruit
Calories 2 T. (30 mL): 7

Cherry Jelly or Topping

1 c.	sour cherries	250 mL
1 c.	water	250 mL
3 T.	granulated sugar replacement	45 mL
1 T.	lo-cal pectin	15 mL

Rinse cherries and remove the stems. Combine cherries and water in saucepan. Bring to boil, reduce heat, and simmer 5 minutes. Strain; reserve juice. Add sugar replacement and pectin to 1 c. (250 mL) of juice, adding extra water, if necessary, to make up the juice. Stir to completely blend and return to heat. Bring back to boil, boil for 1 minute and then remove from heat. Cool slightly. Pour into serving dish or jelly jar; chill.

Microwave: Follow directions using large bowl. Cook on High.

Yield: ¾ c. (190 mL)
Exchange 1 T. (15 mL): ⅕ fruit
Calories 1 T. (15 mL): 8

CREPES AND DESSERT OMELETS

Rich Crepes

3	eggs	3
dash	salt	dash
2 T.	liquid shortening	30 mL
1¼ c.	flour	310 mL
½ c.	evaporated skimmed milk	125 mL
1 c.	water	500 mL

Place eggs in blender; whip to mix well. Add salt, shortening, flour, milk and water. Whip to blend thoroughly. Allow to rest 1 hour at room temperature before using. Cook in crepe pan according to manufacturer's directions.

Yield: Thirty-six 6-in. (15-cm) crepes
Exchange 1 crepe: ¼ full-fat milk
Calories 1 crepe: 30

Compote Crepes

16	Rich Crepes (p. 96)	16
1 recipe	Red Fruit Compote (p. 91)	1 recipe
1 c.	lo-cal whipped topping (prepared)	250 mL

Cook the crepes. Place heaping ¼ c. (60 mL) Red Fruit Compote into center of each crepe. Fold crepe in half, then fold in half again, making a pie-wedge shape. Top with scant 1 T. (15 mL) topping.

Yield: 16 servings
Exchange 1 serving: ½ bread
                        ½ fat
Calories 1 serving: 80

Blueberry Crepes

12	Rich Crepes (p. 96)	12
2 T.	cornstarch	30 mL
2 T.	granulated sugar replacement	30 mL
dash	salt	dash
1 c.	skim milk	250 mL
1 T.	lemon juice	15 mL
2 t.	vanilla extract	10 mL
2 c.	fresh blueberries (rinsed)	500 mL
1 c.	lo-cal whipped topping (prepared)	250 mL

Reserve crepes. Combine cornstarch, sugar replacement, salt, milk, lemon juice and vanilla in saucepan. Cook and stir over medium heat until slightly thickened; remove from heat. Crush 1 c. (250 mL) of the blueberries and add to cream mixture. Return to heat, and cook and stir until thickened. Cool. Fold in remaining blueberries. Divide evenly between crepes, and fold or roll the crepes. Top each with heaping 1 T. (15 mL) topping.

Yield: 12 servings
Exchange 1 serving: ½ bread
½ fat
Calories 1 serving: 72

Lo-Cal Crepes

2	eggs	2
dash	salt	dash
2 T.	margarine (melted)	30 mL
1¼ c.	flour	310 mL
1 t.	baking powder	5 mL
1¾ c.	water	440 mL

Place eggs in blender; whip to mix well. Add salt, melted margarine, flour, baking powder and water. Whip to blend thoroughly. (Should batter become too thick, add a little extra water; stir to blend.) Cook in crepe pan according to manufacturer's directions.

Yield: 36 6-in. (15-cm) crepes
Exchange 1 crepe: ¼ low-fat milk
Calories 1 crepe: 24

Orange-Suzette Crepes

12	Lo-Cal Crepes (p. 97)	12
2 T.	butter	30 mL
1 c.	orange juice	250 mL
1 T.	lemon juice	15 mL
1 t.	cornstarch	5 mL
2 T.	fresh orange peel (grated)	30 mL

Reserve crepes. Fold crepes into fourths, and place in shallow pan or in serving dishes. Melt butter in small pan. Combine juices and cornstarch in shaker bottle, shaking well to mix. Pour into pan with melted butter; add orange peel. Cook and stir mixture over medium heat until clear and slightly thickened. Pour evenly over crepes, and serve immediately.

Yield: 12 servings
Exchange 1 serving: ⅓ bread
　　　　　　　　　　½ fat
Calories 1 serving: 55

Banana Split Crepes

2	Lo-Cal Crepes (p. 97)	2
1	banana	1
2 t.	granulated brown sugar replacement	10 mL
1 t.	butter (melted)	5 mL
1 T.	Chocolate Topping (p. 137)	15 mL

Reserve crepes. Peel and split banana lengthwise. Place 1 banana half in center of each crepe. Dissolve brown sugar replacement in melted butter and pour over bananas. Roll the crepes, and heat in microwave oven if desired. Top both crepes evenly with Chocolate Topping.

Yield: 2 servings
Exchange 1 serving: 1 bread
　　　　　　　　　　½ fat
Calories 1 serving: 95

Peach Crepes

2	Lo-Cal Crepes (p. 97)	2
1	peach	1
1 t.	lemon juice	5 mL
1 t.	Powdered Sugar Replacement (p. 134)	5 mL

Reserve crepes. Peel and slice peach and toss with lemon juice. Divide peach slices evenly between crepes. Fold or roll crepes. Sift sugar replacement over crepes.

Yield: 2 servings
Exchange 1 serving: ½ bread
⅓ fat
Calories 1 serving: 50

Blintzes

12	Lo-Cal Crepes (p. 97)	12
1 c.	creamed cottage cheese	250 mL
2 T.	granulated sugar replacement	30 mL
1 t.	vanilla extract	5 mL
½ t.	lemon peel (grated)	2 mL
2 T.	Powdered Sugar Replacement (p. 134)	30 mL

Reserve crepes. Combine cottage cheese, granulated sugar replacement, vanilla and lemon peel in mixing bowl. Whip with fork until thoroughly blended. Fill each crepe with heaping 1 T. (15 mL) of cottage cheese filling, roll each one to form blintzes and place in shallow pan. Bake at 350 °F (175 °C) for 15 minutes, or until warm. Sift the powdered sugar replacement over the blintzes.

Microwave: Cook on Medium for 1 minute. Sift the powdered sugar replacement over the blintzes.

Yield: 12 servings
Exchange 1 serving: ⅓ bread
⅓ lean meat
Calories 1 serving: 30

Crepe Cake

12	Lo-Cal Crepes (p. 97)	12
2 c.	unsweetened pumpkin puree	500 mL
3 T.	granulated sugar replacement	45 mL
2	egg yolks (beaten)	2
1 T.	flour	15 mL
½ c.	low-fat milk (2% milkfat)	125 mL
2	egg whites	2
pinch	cream of tartar	pinch

Reserve crepes. Combine pumpkin, sugar replacement, beaten egg yolks, flour and milk in saucepan. Cook and stir over low heat until thickened. Remove from heat; cool slightly. Place 1 crepe on oven-proof plate. Spread crepe with a thin layer of pumpkin mixture. Repeat, using all crepes, and ending with pumpkin layer. Beat egg whites until frothy and add cream of tartar. Beat into stiff peaks. Spread on top of pumpkin layer. Place 4 in. (10 cm) underneath a hot broiler. Broil just until tips of egg whites turn brown. Cut into 6 pie-shaped servings.

Yield: 6 servings
Exchange 1 serving: 1 bread
½ high-fat meat
Calories 1 serving: 128

Sweet Omelet

2	eggs	2
1 t.	granulated sugar replacement or granulated fructose vegetable cooking spray	5 mL
2 t.	Powdered Sugar Replacement (p. 134)	10 mL

Break eggs into bowl or cup, and beat with fork until blended. Beat in granulated sugar replacement. Coat small frying pan with vegetable spray. Heat until warm. Add eggs and cook them over low heat until slightly set. Run fork or spatula around edge of omelet. Tilt pan slightly to allow excess egg to seep under to pan. Continue cooking until firm. Fold in half; remove to heated serving plate. Sift 2 t. (10 mL) powdered sugar replacement over omelet.

Yield: 1 serving
Exchange with sugar replacement: 2 medium-fat meat
Calories with sugar replacement: 171
Exchange with fructose: 2 medium-fat meat
Calories with fructose: 181

Fillings for Sweet Omelet

APPLE: 1 small apple (peeled and sliced)
           ½ t. (2 mL) granulated sugar replacement
           ¼ t. (1 mL) cinnamon
           ¼ t. (1 mL) vanilla extract

Combine apple slices with remaining ingredients. Toss to coat. When omelet is still slightly soft, spread apple mixture in center of eggs. Fold in half and cook until set.

Yield: 1 serving
Exchange: 1 fruit
           plus omelet
Calories: 70
           plus omelet

BLUEBERRY: ½ c. (125 mL) fresh blueberries (rinsed)
             ½ t. (2 mL) almond extract

When omelet is still slightly soft, spread blueberries in center of eggs. Sprinkle with almond extract. Fold in half and cook until set.

Yield: 1 serving
Exchange: 1 fruit
           plus omelet
Calories: 40
           plus omelet

1 T. (15 mL) dark rum (heated)

Pour heated rum around sides of cooked omelet on serving dish. Ignite.

Yield: 1 serving
Exchange: Same as omelet
Calories: Same as omelet

BERRY-CHERRY: 5 strawberries (sliced)
                 10 raspberries
                 4 Bing cherries (pitted and halved)

When omelet is still slightly soft, spread fruit in center of eggs. Fold in half and cook until set.

Yield: 1 serving
Exchange: 1 fruit
          plus omelet
Calories: 40
          plus omelet

Plum Whip Crepes

8	Lo-Cal Crepes (p. 97)	8
1 recipe	Fresh Plum Whip (p. 94)	1 recipe
¼ c.	Powdered Sugar Replacement (p. 134)	60 mL

Cook the crepes. Divide Plum Whip evenly into center of crepes and fold or roll the crepe. Dust with powdered sugar replacement.

Yield: 8 servings
Exchange 1 serving: ½ bread   ½ fruit
                        ½ fat   **or**   ¼ low-fat milk
Calories 1 serving: 57

PASTRIES, STRUDELS AND TORTES

Mizithropeta

1 c.	dry cottage cheese	250 mL
2 T.	granulated sugar replacement	30 mL
½ t.	vanilla extract	2 mL
½ t.	lemon rind (grated)	2 mL
1	egg	1
10	phyllo leaves	10
¼ c.	butter (melted)	60 mL
1	egg white (slightly beaten)	1
4 t.	Powdered Sugar Replacement (p. 134)	20 mL
2 t.	cinnamon	10 mL

Combine cottage cheese, granulated sugar replacement, vanilla, lemon rind and the whole egg in bowl. Stir to completely blend. Cut each phyllo leaf into three pieces and fold each piece in half. Combine melted butter and slightly beaten egg white in cup, beating with fork to blend. Brush each folded phyllo piece lightly with butter mixture. Place heaping 1 T. (15 mL) of cheese mixture in center of each piece, and fold phyllo leaves into triangular shape. Lightly brush top of triangle with butter mixture, and place on lightly greased cookie sheets. Bake at 350 °F (175 °C) for 10 to 12 minutes, or until lightly browned. Remove to cooling rack; cool. Combine powdered sugar replacement and cinnamon in cup, stir to mix, and sprinkle over triangles.

Yield: 30 triangles
Exchange 2 triangles: ⅓ low-fat milk
Calories 2 triangles: 68

Royal Pastry

½ lb.	phyllo leaves	225 g
¼ c.	butter (melted)	60 mL
1	egg white (slightly beaten)	1
5	eggs (separated)	5
3 T.	granulated sugar replacement	45 mL
1 t.	rum flavoring	5 mL
½ t.	cinnamon	2 mL
¼ t.	nutmeg	1 mL
1 c.	walnuts (finely ground)	250 mL
½ c.	bread crumbs (finely ground)	125 mL

Place one-sixth of the phyllo leaves on lightly greased 9 × 13-in. (23 × 33-cm) baking dish. Combine melted butter and the slightly beaten egg white in cup; beat with fork to blend. Brush phyllo leaves lightly with some of the butter mixture. Repeat entire procedure 2 more times, using a total of half of the phyllo leaves. Beat the 5 egg yolks with sugar replacement until light, thick and lemon-colored. Add rum flavoring, cinnamon, nutmeg, walnuts and bread crumbs; fold to mix. Beat the 5 egg whites until stiff and then fold into walnut mixture. Spread evenly over phyllo leaves in baking dish. On towel, brush one-third of remaining phyllo leaves with melted butter mixture. Lay on top of walnut mixture. Repeat 2 more times with remaining phyllo leaves. Bake at 350 °F (175 °C) for 40 to 45 minutes, or until golden brown. While warm, score into 4 slices on short side and 6 slices on long side to form 24 squares. Score each square into a triangle.

Yield: 48 triangles
Exchange 1 triangle: ½ fruit, ½ high-fat meat
Calories 1 triangle: 64

Cream Puff Pastry

1 c.	water	250 mL
¼ c.	margarine	60 mL
dash	salt	dash
1 c.	flour	250 mL
4	eggs	4

Combine water, margarine and salt in medium saucepan. Cook and stir over high heat until boiling; reduce heat. Add flour and cook and stir over medium heat until mixture comes clean from sides of pan and forms ball in center. Remove from heat; cool slightly. With spoon, electric beater or food processor, add eggs, one at a time. Beat after each addition until batter is smooth and glossy.

FOR CREAM PUFFS: Drop tablespoonfuls onto lightly greased baking sheets. Bake at 425 °F (220 °C) for 15 minutes; reduce heat to 350 °F (175 °C) and bake 25 minutes longer, or until puffs are free of moisture beads. (Puff pastry will collapse if removed from oven early.) Remove from oven. Remove tops or cut into sides to allow hot air to escape; cool completely.

FOR ÉCLAIRS: Spoon pastry batter into pastry bag fitted with ½-in. (1.25-cm) tube. Shape batter into 1 × 4-in. (2 × 10-cm) strips. Bake as for cream puffs.

FILLINGS: Fill with flavored creams or puddings.

Yield: 10 puffs or éclairs
Exchange for 1 puff or éclair: ⅔ full-fat milk
plus filling exchange
Calories for 1 puff or éclair: 114
plus filling calories

Blueberry Bumpkins

1 c.	flour	250 mL
1 T.	granulated sugar replacement	15 mL
2 t.	baking powder	10 mL
dash	salt	dash
2 T.	liquid vegetable shortening	30 mL
1	egg	1
¼ c.	milk	60 mL
⅓ c.	blueberries (fresh or well drained)	90 mL

Combine flour, sugar replacement, baking powder and salt in mixing bowl. Add shortening, egg and milk, stirring just to blend. Fold in blueberries. Drop mixture by tablespoonfuls onto greased baking sheet, and bake at 400 °F (200 °C) for 15 to 20 minutes.

Yield: 7 servings
Exchange 1 serving: 1 bread, ½ fat
Calories 1 serving: 87

Mutzenmandein

2 c.	flour	500 mL
2 t.	baking powder	10 mL
¼ c.	granulated sugar replacement	60 mL
3	eggs	3
1 t.	rum extract	5 mL
½ t.	almond extract	2 mL
⅓ c.	margarine (cold)	90 mL
2 T.	water	30 mL
	oil for deep-fat frying	

Combine flour and baking powder in sifter; sift twice. Pour into large bowl, pushing flour mixture up the sides of the bowl, and add sugar replacement, eggs and flavorings to center well. Push and work flour into egg mixture. Add cold margarine and work into crumbs. Add water, only if needed to make smooth, firm dough. Chill slightly. Roll out ½ in. (1 cm) thick on lightly floured board, and cut into 2 × 1-in. (5 × 2-cm) rectangles. With sharp knife, cut each rectangle lengthwise into small strips. Fry in hot, deep fat (365 °F or 180 °C) until golden brown. Remove with slotted spoon to absorbent paper.

Yield: 32 pastries
Exchange 1 pastry: ⅓ bread
                     ½ fat
Calories 1 pastry: 50

Pastry Cups

1	egg	1
dash	salt	dash
½ c.	skim milk	125 mL
1 t.	vanilla extract	5 mL
½ c.	flour	125 mL
	oil for deep-fat frying	

Combine egg and salt in mixing bowl; beat to blend thoroughly. Add milk, vanilla and flour, beating just to blend and smooth. Heat rosette cup iron in hot deep fat (365 °F or 180 °C), and shake off excess oil. Dip into batter to within ¼ in. (8 mm) of top of iron. Return to hot oil; cover iron completely with oil. Fry until golden brown. Remove to absorbent paper.

Yield: 10 pastry cups
Exchange 1 pastry cup: ⅓ bread
Calories 1 pastry cup: 34

Apple Crisp I

6	baking apples	6
½ c.	water	125 mL
2 t.	vanilla extract	10 mL
¾ c.	flour	190 mL
2 T.	granulated brown sugar replacement	30 mL
	or granulated fructose	
1 t.	cinnamon	5 mL
¼ c.	margarine	60 mL

Wash, peel and slice apples. Place on bottom of 8-in. (20-cm) square baking dish, and add water and vanilla. Combine flour, sugar replacement, cinnamon and margarine in bowl or food processor. Work with pastry wire or steel blade into crumbs. Sprinkle crumbs evenly over top of apple slices. Bake at 375 °F (190 °C) for 30 to 35 minutes.

Yield: 9 servings
Exchange 1 serving with sugar replacement: 2 fruit
1 fat
Calories 1 serving with sugar replacement: 126
Exchange 1 serving with fructose: 2 fruit
1 fat
Calories 1 serving with fructose: 135

Apple Crisp II

1	cooking apple (peeled and sliced)	1
1 t.	orange juice	5 mL
2 t.	granulated sugar replacement	10 mL
2 T.	cornflakes (crushed)	30 mL
1 t.	margarine	5 mL

Place apple slices in small baking dish. Sprinkle with orange juice, sugar replacement and crushed cornflakes; top with margarine. Bake at 350 °F (175 °C) for 20 to 25 minutes.

Microwave: Cook on High for 3 to 4 minutes. Hold 2 minutes.

Yield: 1 serving
Exchange: 1 fruit
　　　　　 1 fat
　　　　　 ⅓ bread
Calories: 109

Date Strudel

½ c.	dates (cut up)	125 mL
1 c.	water	250 mL
1 T.	cornstarch	15 mL
¼ c.	margarine	60 mL
⅓ lb.	phyllo leaves	150 g
	bread crumbs (fine)	

Combine dates, water and cornstarch in saucepan. Cook and stir until very thick; remove from heat. Melt margarine. Place two phyllo leaves, side by side, on a lightly dampened, lightly bread-crumbed cloth. Brush leaves lightly with melted margarine. Lay a second leaf on top of each leaf. Brush each layer lightly with melted margarine. Repeat using all of the leaves. Place date filling 2 in. (5 cm) in from long edges. Fold long edges in over the filling. Fold over the ends. Roll up dough, jelly-roll fashion. Score top into 10 pieces with a sharp knife or scissors and place on greased cookie sheet. Bake at 350 °F (175 °C) for 25 minutes, or until lightly browned.

Yield: 10 pieces
Exchange 1 piece: 1 bread
　　　　　　　　 ½ fat
Calories 1 piece: 100

Apple-Walnut Strudel

2	apples	2
⅓ c.	walnuts (chopped)	90 mL
¼ t.	lemon juice	1 mL
¼ c.	margarine	60 mL
⅓ lb.	phyllo leaves	150 g
	bread crumbs	

Peel, core and chop apples. Combine apples, walnuts and lemon juice in mixing bowl; fold to mix. Melt margarine. Place 2 phyllo leaves on a lightly dampened, lightly bread-crumbed cloth. Brush leaves lightly with melted margarine. Lay a second leaf on top of each leaf. Brush each layer lightly with melted margarine. Repeat using all the leaves. Place apple filling 2 in. (5 cm) in from long edges. Fold long edges in over the filling. Fold over the ends. Roll up dough, jelly-roll fashion. Score top into 10 pieces with a sharp knife or scissors and place on greased cookie sheet. Bake at 350 °F (175 °C) for 25 minutes, or until lightly browned.

Yield: 10 pieces
Exchange 1 piece: ½ bread
1 fat
Calories 1 piece: 108

Grape Tarts

10	Pastry Cups (p. 106)	10
2 T.	cornstarch	30 mL
2 T.	granulated sugar replacement	30 mL
dash	salt	dash
1⅓ c.	unsweetened orange juice	340 mL
2 c.	seedless green grapes	500 mL

Prepare pastry cups. Combine cornstarch, sugar replacement and salt in saucepan. Slowly add orange juice; whip to blend completely. Cook and stir over medium heat until mixture is thickened. Remove from heat, cooling slightly, and fold in grapes. Spoon into pastry cups. Refrigerate at least 1 hour, or until chilled.

Yield: 10 servings
Exchange 1 serving: ½ bread
½ fruit
Calories 1 serving: 61

Cherry Schaum Torte

2	egg whites	2
1 t.	granulated fructose	5 mL
1 t.	white vinegar	5 mL
1 t.	white vanilla extract	5 mL
1-lb. can	sour cherries with juice	450-g can
2 t.	liquid fructose	10 mL
2 t.	cornstarch	10 mL

CRUST: Beat egg whites until stiff. Sprinkle granulated fructose on top and beat well. Continue to beat while adding vinegar and vanilla. Beat until egg whites are very stiff and have lost their gloss. Spread into greased 8-in. (20-cm) pie pan. Bake at 250 °F (125 °C) for 1 hour. Cool completely.

FILLING: Drain cherries thoroughly. Combine cherry juice, liquid fructose and cornstarch in saucepan. Cook over medium heat until clear and thickened; remove from heat. Cool slightly. Fold in cherries; cool completely. Pour into cooled crust.

Yield: 6 servings
Exchange 1 serving: ½ bread
Calories 1 serving: 45

Midnight Torte

½ c.	solid shortening	125 mL
½ c.	granulated sugar replacement	125 mL
2 T.	cold water	30 mL
3	eggs	3
2¼ c.	cake flour	560 mL
⅔ c.	cocoa	180 mL
1¼ t.	baking soda	6 mL
½ t.	baking powder	2 mL
1 t.	salt	5 mL
1⅓ c.	water	340 mL
1 t.	vanilla extract	5 mL
2 t.	almond extract	10 mL
½ c.	Cherry Topping (p. 95)	125 mL
¼ c.	Powdered Sugar Replacement (p. 134)	60 mL

Cream the shortening until fluffy and gradually beat in granulated

110

sugar replacement, 2 T. (30 mL) cold water and eggs, one at a time. Combine cake flour, cocoa, baking soda, baking powder and salt in sifter. Combine 1⅓ c. (340 mL) water and extracts in bowl or pitcher. Sift flour mixture alternately with water into creamed mixture. Beat until blended. Pour evenly into four 9-in. (23-cm) round cake pans, well greased and floured. Bake at 350 °F (175 °C) for 15 to 20 minutes, or until done. Remove from pans; cool completely. Spread bottom cake layer with one-third of cherry topping. Add second cake layer and one-third of the topping; repeat. Top with final cake layer. Dust with sifted powdered sugar replacement.

Yield: 20 servings
Exchange 1 serving: 1 bread
Calories 1 serving: 103

Frankfurt Torte

2½ c.	cake flour	625 mL
dash	salt	dash
⅓ c.	granulated brown sugar replacement	90 mL
1 T.	baking powder	15 mL
¼ c.	margarine	60 mL
2 t.	baking soda	10 mL
2 t.	water	10 mL
¾ c.	buttermilk	190 mL
¼ c.	Powdered Sugar Replacement (p. 134)	60 mL

Combine cake flour, salt, brown sugar replacement and baking powder in bowl. Add margarine; work into crumbs. Reserve 1 c. (250 mL) crumbs for topping. Combine baking soda and water, stirring to dissolve. Add buttermilk and baking soda water to remaining crumbs; stir to completely blend. Pour into 9 × 5-in. (23 × 13-cm) well-greased loaf pan and sprinkle with reserved crumbs. Bake at 350 °F (175 °C) for 50 to 60 minutes, or until done, and then let cool. Sprinkle sifted powdered sugar replacement over top.

Yield: 16 servings
Exchange 1 serving: 1 bread
                      ⅗ fat
Calories 1 serving: 88

German Torte

½ c.	butter	125 mL
¼ c.	granulated sugar replacement	60 mL
2 T.	granulated brown sugar replacement	30 mL
3	eggs	3
2 t.	vanilla extract	10 mL
dash	salt	dash
1½ c.	flour	375 mL
½ c.	cornstarch	125 mL
2 t.	baking powder	10 mL
½ c.	skim milk	125 mL
¼ c.	lemon juice	60 mL
½ c.	Strawberry Preserves or Topping (p. 95)	125 mL

Cream the butter and sugar replacements until light and fluffy. Add eggs, one at a time, beating constantly. Beat in vanilla and salt. Combine flour, cornstarch and baking powder in sifter; in a bowl or pitcher, combine milk and lemon juice. Add flour alternately with lemon–milk mixture to batter; beat constantly. Pour into well-greased and floured ring mould. Bake at 350 °F (175 °C) for 50 to 60 minutes, or until done. Cool 10 minutes, remove from pan to cooling rack and cool completely. Pierce into center of torte, around the entire ring, with fork or long skewer. Place torte on serving plate. Slightly heat Strawberry Topping and slowly pour over entire surface of torte; topping will sink through the holes and into the torte, giving it more flavor.

Yield: 20 servings
Exchange 1 serving: ⅔ bread
1 fat
Calories 1 serving: 96

PIES

Fine-Crumb Pie Shell

1¼ c.	fine crumbs (graham cracker, dry cereal or zwieback)	300 mL
3 T.	margarine (melted)	45 mL
1 T.	water	15 mL
	spices (optional)	
	granulated sugar replacement (optional)	

Combine crumbs with melted margarine and water; add spices and sugar replacement, if desired. Spread dough evenly in 8- to 10-in. (20- to 25-cm) pie pan, pressing firmly onto sides and bottom. Either chill until set, or bake at 325 °F (165 °C) for 8 to 10 minutes.

Yield: 8 servings
Exchange 1 serving graham cracker: 1 bread
1 fat
Calories 1 serving graham cracker: 85
Exchange 1 serving dry cereal: ½ bread
1 fat
Calories 1 serving dry cereal: 64
Exchange 1 serving zwieback: ½ bread
1 fat
Calories 1 serving zwieback: 70

Basic Pie Shell

⅓ c.	shortening	90 mL
1 c.	flour (sifted)	250 mL
¼ t.	salt	1 mL
2 to 4 T.	ice water	30 to 60 mL

Chill shortening. Cut shortening into flour and salt until mixture forms crumbs. Add ice water, 1 T. (15 mL) at a time, and flip mixture around in bowl until a ball forms. Wrap ball in plastic wrap and chill at least 1 hour. Roll to fit 9-in. (23-cm) pie pan. Fill with pie filling or prick with fork. Bake at 425 °F (220 °C) for 10 to 12 minutes or until firm, or leave unbaked.

Yield: 8 servings
Exchange 1 serving: 1 bread, 1 fat
Calories 1 serving: 120

Apple Pandowdy

6	cooking apples	6
2 T.	flour	30 mL
¼ t.	salt	1 mL
2 t.	white vinegar	10 mL
½ c.	water	125 mL
1 t.	vanilla extract	5 mL
1 t.	butter	5 mL
2 T.	granulated brown sugar replacement	30 mL

Peel, core and slice apples; place in bottom of 9-in. (23-cm) square baking dish. Combine flour, salt, vinegar and water in saucepan and cook over medium heat for 5 minutes. Remove from heat. Stir in vanilla, butter and brown sugar replacement, and pour mixture over apple slices.

CRUMB TOPPING:

½ c.	flour	125 mL
1 t.	baking powder	5 mL
¼ t.	salt	1 mL
1 T.	solid shortening	15 mL
¼ c.	skim milk	60 mL

Combine flour, baking powder, salt and shortening in bowl or food processor; work into fine crumbs. Stir in milk just until mixture is moistened. Drop by teaspoonfuls onto apple mixture. Bake at 400 °F (200 °C) for 30 to 35 minutes, or until lightly browned.

Yield: 9 servings
Exchange 1 serving: 2 fruit
Calories 1 serving: 82

Cherry Pie

1 recipe	unbaked Basic Pie Shell (p. 114)	1 recipe
two 16-oz. cans	tart sour cherries with juice	two 448-g cans
3 T.	cornstarch	45 mL
¼ c.	granulated sugar replacement or granulated fructose	60 mL
¼ t.	almond extract	1 mL
dash	salt	dash
	red food color	

Prepare pie dough; wrap ball in plastic wrap and chill at least 1 hour.

Drain cherries; reserve ½ c. (125 mL) of cherry juice. Combine reserved cherry juice, cornstarch, sugar replacement, almond extract and salt in saucepan. Cook and stir over medium heat until slightly thickened, though the mixture will not be clear. Add a few drops of red food color, fold in cherries, and allow filling to rest while rolling out dough.

Roll out pie dough on lightly floured surface into a circle larger than a 9-in. (23-cm) pie plate. Place in pie plate, securing dough to plate by pressing edge with tongs of a wet fork. Cut away excess and roll it out thinly. Cut into 8 heart-shaped designs with cookie cutter. Prick with fork.

Pour cherry filling into pie shell. Arrange hearts evenly on top of cherry filling. Bake at 425 °F (220 °C) for 40 to 50 minutes, or until crust is browned.

Yield: 8 servings
Exchange 1 serving with sugar replacement: 1½ fruit
plus pie shell exchange
Calories 1 serving with sugar replacement: 58
plus pie shell calories
Exchange 1 serving with fructose: 2 fruit
plus pie shell exchange
Calories 1 serving with fructose: 73
plus pie shell calories

Apple Pie

9-in.	unbaked Basic Pie Shell (p. 114)	23-cm
2 t.	lemon juice	10 mL
10	apples (peeled and sliced)	10
2 T.	granulated sugar replacement or granulated fructose	30 mL
1 T.	flour	15 mL
1 t.	cinnamon	5 mL
½ t.	nutmeg	2 mL

Prepare, but do not bake, pie shell. Sprinkle lemon juice over sliced apples, tossing to coat, and pour into pie shell. Combine sugar replacement, flour, cinnamon and nutmeg in cup and stir to mix. Sprinkle over apples. Bake at 425 °F (220 °C) for 35 to 40 minutes.

Yield: 8 servings
Exchange 1 serving with sugar replacement: 2 fruit
plus pie shell exchange
Calories 1 serving with sugar replacement: 103
plus pie shell calories
Exchange 1 serving with fructose: 2⅓ fruit
plus pie shell exchange
Calories 1 serving with fructose: 113
plus pie shell calories

Plum Pie

9-in.	unbaked Basic Pie Shell (p. 114)	23-cm
2 lbs.	fresh red plums	900 g
½ c.	water	125 mL
¼ c.	granulated sugar replacement	60 mL
¼ c.	cornstarch	60 mL
¼ t.	salt	1 mL
1 recipe	Crumb Topping, optional (p. 138)	1 recipe

Prepare, but do not bake, pie shell. Pit and quarter plums, and combine with ¼ c. (60 mL) of the water in saucepan; bring to boil. Reduce heat, cover and simmer 3 to 4 minutes. Combine remaining ¼ c. (60 mL) water, the sugar replacement, cornstarch and salt in shaker bottle, shaking to blend. Pour into hot plum mixture. Cook over low heat, stirring constantly, until thick and clear. Remove from heat; cool. Pour into unbaked pie shell, topping with Crumb Topping, if desired. Bake at 400 °F (200 °C) for 30 minutes.

Yield: 8 servings
Exchange 1 serving without crumb topping: 2½ fruit
plus pie shell exchange
Calories 1 serving without crumb topping: 79
plus pie shell calories
Exchange 1 serving with crumb topping: 2 fruit
plus pie shell exchange
Calories 1 serving with crumb topping: 112
plus pie shell calories

Coconut Pie

9-in.	baked Basic Pie Shell (p. 114)	23-cm
1½ c.	unsweetened coconut (grated)	375 mL
3 c.	milk	750 mL
3 T.	cornstarch	45 mL
1 t.	white vanilla extract	5 mL
1 pkg.	lo-cal whipped topping mix	1 pkg.
1 T.	Powdered Sugar Replacement (p. 134)	15 mL

Prepare and bake pie shell. Reserve 2 T. (30 mL) coconut. Combine ¾ c. (190 mL) of the remaining coconut, 2 c. (500 mL) of the milk and the cornstarch in blender, blending until thoroughly mixed. Pour into saucepan. Cook and stir over medium heat until thickened. Add remaining coconut and vanilla. Allow to completely cool. Place the 2 T. (30 mL) of reserved coconut in baking pan, and bake at 350 °F (175 °C) until lightly toasted. Shake occasionally. Put the cooled coconut-milk mixture in baked pie shell. Prepare topping as directed on package. After stiff peaks form, add powdered sugar replacement, beating until smooth. Spread on top of coconut pie; sprinkle with toasted coconut. Refrigerate.

Yield: 8 servings
Exchange 1 serving: 1 high-fat meat
plus pie shell exchange
Calories 1 serving: 102
plus pie shell calories

Blueberry Pie

9-in.	unbaked Basic Pie Shell (p. 114)	23-cm
1 qt.	fresh blueberries (rinsed)	1 L
3 T.	cornstarch	45 mL
3 T.	granulated sugar replacement or granulated fructose	45 mL

Prepare, but do not bake, pie shell. Combine blueberries, cornstarch and sugar replacement in bowl, tossing to coat, and pour into pie shell. Bake at 425 °F (220 °C) for 35 to 40 minutes.

Yield: 8 servings
Exchange 1 serving with sugar replacement: 1 fruit
plus pie shell exchange
Calories 1 serving with sugar replacement: 48
plus pie shell calories
Exchange 1 serving with fructose: 1⅓ fruit
plus pie shell exchange
Calories 1 serving with fructose: 58
plus pie shell calories

Mincemeat Pie

9-in.	unbaked Basic Pie Shell (p. 114)	23-cm
½ lb.	beef stew meat	250 g
2 medium	apples	2 medium
1	orange with rind	1
½	lemon with rind	½
¼ lb.	suet	125 g
½ c.	raisins	125 mL
½ c.	currants	125 mL
3 T.	granulated sugar replacement	45 mL
½ c.	orange juice	125 mL
½ t.	salt	2 mL
¼ t.	nutmeg	1 mL
dash	cinnamon	dash
dash	mace	dash

Prepare, but do not bake, pie shell. Place stew meat in covered saucepan; cover meat with water. Place over medium heat and cook about 1 hour, or until very tender. Drain thoroughly. Core apples and slice; cut orange and lemon into small pieces. Combine beef, suet, apples, orange and lemon in food processor or food chopper, chopping into coarse-meal consistency. Pour back into saucepan, add remaining ingredients, cover and simmer over low heat for 1 hour. Pour into unbaked pie shell. Bake at 400 °F (200 °C) for 25 minutes.

Yield: 8 servings
Exchange 1 serving: 1 bread
                         1 high-fat meat
                         2 fat
                         plus pie shell exchange
Calories 1 serving: 284
                         plus pie shell calories

Raisin Pecan Pie

9-in.	unbaked Basic Pie Shell (p. 114)	23-cm
1½ c.	evaporated skimmed milk	375 mL
¼ c.	granulated sugar replacement	60 mL
1 T.	butter	15 mL
4	eggs	4
2 t.	cornstarch	10 mL
¼ t.	salt	1 mL
1 c.	pecans (chopped)	250 mL
1 t.	vanilla extract	5 mL
⅓ c.	raisins	90 mL

Prepare, but do not bake, pie shell. Combine milk, sugar replacement, butter, eggs, cornstarch and salt in heavy saucepan. Cook and stir over medium-low heat until well blended and slightly thickened. Remove from heat, stir in pecans and vanilla and allow filling to rest 10 minutes. Sprinkle raisins on bottom of unbaked pie shell and pour pecan mixture over them. Bake at 375 °F (190 °C) for 45 to 50 minutes, or until knife inserted in center comes out clean.

Yield: 8 servings
Exchange 1 serving: 1 full-fat milk
                         1 fat
                         plus pie shell exchange
Calories 1 serving: 199
                         plus pie shell calories

Chocolate Rum Pie

9-in.	baked Basic Pie Shell (p. 114)	23-cm
1 env.	unflavored gelatin	1 env.
1 c.	skim milk	250 mL
2	egg yolks	2
2 T.	granulated sugar replacement	30 mL
dash	salt	dash
¼ c.	cocoa	60 mL
2 t.	rum flavoring	10 mL
2	egg whites	2
1 T.	liquid sugar replacement	15 mL
2 c.	lo-cal whipped topping (prepared)	500 mL

Prepare and bake pie shell. Combine gelatin, milk, egg yolks, granulated sugar replacement, salt and cocoa in heavy saucepan. Cook and stir over low heat until completely blended and slightly thickened. Remove from heat. Stir in rum flavoring and chill until partially set. Beat egg whites and liquid sugar replacement into stiff peaks and fold into cooled chocolate mixture. Layer chocolate mixture and topping into baked pie shell, ending with topping. Chill until firm.

Yield: 8 servings
Exchange 1 serving: ½ high-fat meat
⅓ fruit
plus pie shell exchange
Calories 1 serving: 74
plus pie shell calories

Tart Rhubarb Soufflé Pie

9-in.	unbaked Basic Pie Shell (p. 114)	23-cm
1 qt.	rhubarb, cut into 1-in. (2.5-cm) pieces	1 L
⅓ c.	water	90 mL
1 env.	unsweetened strawberry drink mix	1 env.
2 T.	cornstarch	30 mL
¼ c.	granulated sugar replacement	60 mL
2	egg whites	2

Prepare, but do not bake, pie shell. Combine rhubarb and water in saucepan, and cook over medium heat until rhubarb is tender. Pour into blender or food processor, add strawberry drink mix, cornstarch and sugar replacement, and puree. Refrigerate to chill completely. Beat egg whites until stiff; beat rhubarb mixture to loosen. Blend egg whites into rhubarb mixture and pour into pie shell, spreading evenly. Attach a 2-in. (5-cm) collar of flour-dusted waxed paper. Preheat oven to 400 °F (200 °C); reduce heat to 375 °F (190 °C). Place pie in lower third of oven. Bake for 30 or 35 minutes. Insert wire cake tester in center; soufflé is done if tester comes out clean. (Place waxed paper over collar to keep top from getting too brown.)

Yield: 8 servings
Exchange 1 serving: Negligible
plus pie shell exchange
Calories 1 serving: 12
plus pie shell calories

Butterscotch Pie

9-in.	baked Basic Pie Shell (p. 114)	23-cm
¾ c.	granulated brown sugar replacement	190 mL
2 T.	flour	30 mL
1 c.	cold skim milk	250 mL
2	eggs, separated	2
2 T.	margarine	30 mL
1 t.	vanilla extract	5 mL
pinch	salt	pinch
2 t.	granulated sugar replacement	10 mL

Prepare and bake pie shell. Combine brown sugar replacement, flour, milk, egg yolks, margarine, vanilla extract and salt. Cook over medium heat until mixture is thick, stirring constantly; pour pudding into baked pie shell. Whip egg whites until soft peaks form; add granulated sugar replacement, and whip until thick and stiff. Top pudding with meringue, carefully sealing edges. Bake at 350 °F (175 °C) for 12 to 15 minutes, or until delicately brown.

Yield: 8 servings
Exchange 1 serving: ½ milk
1 fat
plus pie shell exchange
Calories 1 serving: 62
plus pie shell calories

Pumpkin Cheese Pie

9-in.	unbaked Basic Pie Shell (p. 114)	23-cm

CHEESE LAYER:

8-oz. pkg.	cream cheese (softened)	220-g pkg.
2 T.	granulated sugar replacement	30 mL
1 t.	vanilla extract	5 mL
1	egg	1

PIE LAYER:

1½ c.	cooked pumpkin (unsweetened)	375 mL
1 c.	evaporated skimmed milk	250 mL
2	eggs	2
2 T.	granulated sugar replacement	30 mL
1 t.	cinnamon	5 mL
¼ t.	ginger	1 mL
¼ t.	nutmeg	1 mL

Prepare, but do not bake, pie shell. Combine cream cheese, sugar replacement, vanilla and 1 egg in mixing bowl; stir to mix well. Spread in bottom of unbaked pie shell. Combine pumpkin, milk, 2 eggs, sugar replacement and spices in a mixing bowl or food processor, beating to blend thoroughly. Carefully pour over cheese layer. Bake at 350 °F (175 °C) for 65 to 70 minutes, or until knife inserted in center comes out clean.

Microwave: Cook on Medium for 20 to 25 minutes, or until edges are set and center is soft but not runny. Allow to rest 15 to 20 minutes before serving.

Yield: 8 servings
Exchange 1 serving: 1 high-fat meat
1 fat
½ fruit
plus pie shell exchange
Calories 1 serving: 173
plus pie shell calories

CAKES

Carrot Cake

1 c.	liquid shortening	250 mL
2T.	granulated fructose or	30 mL
	granulated sugar replacement	
4	eggs	4
½ c.	water	125 mL
2 c.	flour	500 mL
1 t.	baking powder	5 mL
1 t.	baking soda	5 mL
2 t.	cinnamon	10 mL
1 t.	nutmeg	5 mL
½ t.	salt	2 mL
½ c.	pecans (chopped)	125 mL
3 c.	carrots (grated)	750 mL

Beat shortening, sugar replacement and eggs until lemon colored. Add water, flour, baking powder, baking soda, cinnamon, nutmeg and salt, beating well. Stir in pecans and carrots. Pour into well-greased and floured 3-qt. (3-L) tube pan. Bake at 350 °F (175 °C) for 30 to 40 minutes, or until done.

Microwave: Cook on Medium for 15 to 17 minutes. Allow to rest 5 minutes before removing from pan.

Yield: 16 servings
Exchange 1 serving with fructose: 1 bread
3 fat
Calories 1 serving with fructose: 229
Exchange 1 serving with sugar replacement: 1 bread
3 fat
Calories 1 serving with sugar replacement: 220

Sponge Cake

4	eggs (separated)	4
3T.	granulated sugar replacement	45 mL
½ c.	hot water	125 mL
1½ t.	vanilla extract	7 mL
1½ c.	cake flour (sifted)	375 mL
¼ t.	salt	1 mL
¼ t.	baking powder	1 mL

With electric beater, beat egg yolks and sugar replacement until thick and lemon colored. Beat in hot water and vanilla. Combine cake flour, salt and baking powder in sifter; sift and stir into egg yolk mixture. Beat egg whites until stiff and fold into egg yolk mixture. Spoon batter into ungreased 9-in. (23-cm) tube pan. Bake at 325 °F (165 °C) for 55 to 60 minutes, or until cake is done. Invert pan and allow cake to cool at least 1 hour. Remove from pan.

Yield: 16 servings
Exchange 1 serving: ½ bread
Calories 1 serving: 54

Milk Sponge Cake

2	eggs	2
2 T.	granulated sugar replacement or granulated fructose	30 mL
1 c.	cake flour (sifted)	250 mL
1 t.	baking powder	5 mL
1 t.	vanilla extract	5 mL
1 t.	margarine	5 mL
½ c.	hot skim milk	125 mL

Beat eggs and sugar replacement; beat in cake flour, baking powder and vanilla. Melt margarine in hot milk and pour into cake batter, beating just to blend. Pour into 9-in. (23-cm) baking dish. Bake at 350 °F (175 °C) for 30 to 35 minutes, or until done.

Yield: 9 servings
Exchange 1 serving with sugar replacement: 1 fruit
½ medium-fat meat
Calories 1 serving with sugar replacement: 45
Exchange 1 serving with fructose: 1 fruit
½ medium-fat meat
Calories 1 serving with fructose: 48

124

Walnut Sponge Cake

6	eggs (separated)	6
½ c.	cold water	125 mL
½ t.	vanilla extract	3 mL
3 T.	granulated sugar replacement	45 mL
1¼ c.	flour	310 mL
½ t.	cinnamon	3 mL
¼ t.	salt	1 mL
½ c.	walnuts (chopped fine)	125 mL
¾ t.	cream of tartar	4 mL

Beat egg yolks until thick and lemon colored. Add water, vanilla and sugar replacement, beating until light and fluffy. Stir in flour, cinnamon, salt and walnuts. Beat egg whites until foamy and add cream of tartar, beating until stiff peaks are formed. Gently fold egg yolk mixture into stiffly beaten egg whites. Pour into ungreased 9-in. (23-cm) tube pan. Bake at 325 °F (165 °C) for 60 to 70 minutes, or until cake springs back when lightly touched with finger. Invert cake in pan over bottle or wire rack and cool 1 hour before removing from pan.

Yield: 20 servings
Exchange 1 serving: ½ full-fat milk
Calories 1 serving: 69

Chocolate Cake

1½ c.	flour	375 mL
¼ c.	granulated sugar replacement	60 mL
½ c.	unsweetened cocoa	125 mL
1½ t.	baking soda	7 mL
1 t.	salt	5 mL
1 c.	low-fat milk (2% milkfat)	250 mL
⅔ c.	liquid shortening	160 mL
2	eggs	2

Combine all ingredients in large bowl and beat just until blended. Pour into well-greased and floured 13 × 9-in. (33 × 23-cm) cake pan. Bake at 350 °F (175 °C) for 40 to 45 minutes, or until done.

Yield: 24 servings
Exchange 1 serving: ½ bread
    1 fat
Calories 1 serving: 86

Wacky Chocolate Cake

1½ c.	cake flour	375 mL
¼ c.	cocoa	60 mL
2 T.	granulated sugar replacement	30 mL
1 t.	baking soda	5 mL
½ t.	salt	2 mL
1 c.	water	250 mL
1 T.	white vinegar	15 mL
¼ c.	liquid shortening	60 mL
1 t.	vanilla extract	5 mL
1	egg	1

Combine cake flour, cocoa, sugar replacement, baking soda and salt in sifter. Sift into large bowl, add remaining ingredients and beat to mix. Pour into 9-in. (23-cm) square baking dish. Bake at 375 °F (190 °C) for 35 to 40 minutes, or until done.

Microwave: Cook on Medium for 10 to 11 minutes, turning dish a quarter turn every 5 minutes.

Yield: 9 servings
Exchange 1 serving: 1 bread
                       1 fat
Calories 1 serving: 89

Southern Peach Shortcake

2 c.	sliced peaches	500 mL
2 T.	granulated sugar replacement	30 mL
½ t.	almond extract	2 mL
½ t.	cinnamon	2 mL
1 c.	flour	250 mL
2 t.	baking powder	10 mL
dash	salt	dash
2 T.	liquid vegetable shortening	30 mL
1	egg	1
¼ c.	milk	60 mL

Place peaches in bottom of well-greased 8-in. (20-cm) baking dish. Sprinkle with 1 T. (15 mL) of the sugar replacement, the almond extract and cinnamon. Combine flour, remaining 1 T. (15 mL) sugar replacement, baking powder and salt in mixing bowl. Add shortening,

126

egg and milk, stirring just to mix. Spread evenly over peaches. Bake at 400 °F (200 °C) for 30 minutes, or until lightly browned. Invert onto serving plate.

Yield: 9 servings
Exchange 1 serving: 1 bread
½ fat
Calories 1 serving: 102

Sour Cream Spice Cake

⅓ c.	margarine	90 mL
3 T.	granulated brown sugar replacement	3 mL
2	eggs	2
2 t.	cinnamon	10 mL
1 t.	cloves (ground)	5 mL
1 t.	nutmeg	5 mL
2 c.	flour (sifted)	500 mL
1 t.	baking powder	5 mL
1¼ t.	baking soda	4 mL
½ t.	salt	2 mL
½ c.	water	125 mL
1 c.	sour cream	250 mL
½ c.	raisins	125 mL
¼ c.	walnuts (chopped)	60 mL

Cream together margarine and brown sugar replacement; add eggs, beating well. Beat in cinnamon, cloves and nutmeg. Combine flour, baking powder, baking soda and salt in sifter, and beat into creamed mixture alternately with water. Stir in sour cream, raisins and walnuts. Pour into greased and floured 13 × 9-in. (33 × 23-cm) baking pan. Bake at 350 °F (175 °C) for 30 to 35 minutes, or until done.

Microwave: Pour into two 8-in. (20-cm) baking dishes. Cook on Medium for 10 to 12 minutes. Turn dishes a quarter turn every 5 minutes.

Yield: 18 servings
Exchange 1 serving: 1½ bread
1 fat
Calories 1 serving: 124

Applesauce Cake

¾ c.	margarine (soft)	190 mL
3 T.	granulated sugar replacement	45 mL
2	eggs	2
2½ c.	flour	625 mL
1 t.	salt	5 mL
1 t.	cinnamon	5 mL
1 t.	cloves (ground)	5 mL
1 t.	allspice	5 mL
2 t.	baking soda	10 mL
2 c.	unsweetened applesauce	500 mL
¼ c.	water (boiling)	60 mL

Cream together margarine and sugar replacement until light and fluffy; beat in eggs. Sift flour, salt, cinnamon, cloves, allspice and baking soda together. Combine applesauce and boiling water. Add flour mixture alternately with applesauce mixture to the creamed margarine, beating to blend. Pour into well-greased 13 × 9-in. (33 × 23-cm) baking pan. Bake at 350 °F (175 °C) for 45 to 50 minutes, or until done.

Yield: 24 servings
Exchange 1 serving: ½ bread
1 fat
Calories 1 serving: 101

Quick Chocolate Walnut-Filled Cake

CAKE:

2 c.	cake flour	500 mL
½ c.	cocoa	125 mL
3 T.	granulated sugar replacement	45 mL
1 T.	baking powder	15 mL
1¼ c.	milk	310 mL
¼ c.	margarine (soft)	60 mL
2	eggs	2

Combine cake flour, cocoa, sugar replacement and baking powder in sifter. Sift into medium bowl, add remaining ingredients and beat until smooth and creamy. Pour into well-greased and floured 3-qt. (3-L) fluted tube pan.

FILLING:

½ c.	all-purpose flour	125 mL
⅓ c.	walnuts (very finely chopped)	90 mL
⅓ c.	milk	90 mL
1 t.	granulated sugar replacement	5 mL
1 t.	baking powder	5 mL
1 t.	vanilla extract	5 mL

Combine all ingredients in small bowl, mixing with fork until well blended. Spoon in a ring over center of chocolate batter. *Do not touch sides of pan with filling.* Bake at 350 °F (175 °C) for 35 minutes, or until done. Cool in pan 20 to 25 minutes, invert onto cooling rack or plate and cool completely. Frost with favorite glaze.

Yield: 24 servings
Exchange 1 serving: ⅔ bread
½ lean meat
Calories 1 serving: 84

Apricot Pudding Cake

3	eggs (separated)	3
7½-oz. jar	unsweetened apricot puree (baby food)	219-g jar
½ t.	almond extract	3 mL
½ c.	milk	125 mL
⅓ c.	flour (sifted)	90 mL
2 t.	granulated sugar replacement	10 mL

Beat egg yolks. Add apricot puree, almond extract, milk, flour and sugar replacement, beating to blend thoroughly. Stiffly beat the egg whites. Gently and completely fold egg yolk mixture into egg whites. Pour mixture into well-greased 1-qt. (1-L) baking dish, place dish in pan and add ½ in. (15 mm) water to pan. Bake at 325 °F (165 °C) for 30 minutes, or until lightly browned and puffy.

Microwave: Cook on Defrost for 15 to 17 minutes. Turn dish a quarter turn every 5 minutes.

Yield: 6 servings
Exchange 1 serving: 1 bread
½ fat
Calories 1 serving: 113

Lemon Pudding Cake

3	eggs (separated)	3
¼ c.	lemon juice	60 mL
½ c.	milk	125 mL
1 t.	fresh lemon peel (grated)	5 mL
2 T.	granulated sugar replacement	30 mL
dash	salt	dash
⅓ c.	flour (sifted)	90 mL

Beat egg yolks until creamy. Add lemon juice, milk, lemon peel, sugar replacement, salt and flour; beat to blend thoroughly. Stiffly beat the egg whites. Gently fold egg yolk mixture into egg whites. Pour mixture into well-greased 1-qt. (1-L) baking dish, set dish in pan and add ½ in. (15 mm) water to pan. Bake at 325 °F (165 °C) for 30 minutes, or until lightly browned and puffy.

Microwave: Cook on Defrost for 15 to 17 minutes. Turn dish a quarter turn every 5 minutes.

Yield: 6 servings
Exchange 1 serving: ½ bread
  ½ medium-fat meat
Calories 1 serving: 73

Rhubarb Cake

2 c.	flour	500 mL
1 c.	low-fat milk (2% milkfat)	250 mL
¼ c.	margarine (soft)	60 mL
1	egg	1
3 T.	granulated sugar replacement	45 mL
1 t.	baking soda	5 mL
1 t.	lemon juice	5 mL
1 t.	vanilla extract	5 mL
dash	salt	dash
1½ c.	rhubarb (cut fine)	375 mL

Combine flour, milk, margarine, egg, sugar replacement, baking soda, lemon juice, vanilla and salt in large mixing bowl. Stir to blend and then fold in rhubarb. Pour into well-greased and floured 13 × 9-in. (33 × 23-cm) baking pan. Bake at 350 °F (175 °C) for 45 minutes, or until done.

Yield: 24 servings
Exchange 1 serving: ½ bread
½ fat
Calories 1 serving: 60

No-Bake Cherry Cheese Cake

CRUST:

9-in.	Fine-Crumb Pie Shell (p. 113)	23-cm

FILLING:

13-oz. can	evaporated skimmed milk	380-g can
2 T.	cornstarch	30 mL
1 T.	liquid sugar replacement	15 mL
3-oz. pkg.	cream cheese (softened)	90-g pkg.
½ c.	lemon juice	125 mL
1 t.	vanilla extract	5 mL

TOPPING:

1-lb. can	sour cherries with juice	480-g can
2 T.	cornstarch	30 mL
1 T.	liquid sugar replacement	15 mL

Prepare Fine-Crumb Pie Shell; chill.

Combine milk and cornstarch in saucepan; cook and stir over medium heat until thick. *Do not boil.* Remove from heat. Stir in 1 T. (15 mL) sugar replacement; allow to cool. Beat cream cheese until fluffy and add the milk mixture; beat in lemon juice and vanilla. Pour into prepared and chilled pie shell. Chill 2 to 3 hours, or until firm.

Drain sour cherries. Combine cherry juice and cornstarch in saucepan; cook and stir over medium heat until thick and clear. Stir in cherries and sugar replacement; allow to cool. Spread topping evenly over cream cheese and refrigerate.

Yield: 8 servings
Exchange 1 serving: 1 bread
½ high-fat meat
plus pie shell exchange
Calories 1 serving: 112
plus pie shell calories

131

Banana Pudding Cake

3	egg yolks	3
2	bananas (very ripe)	2
1 t.	vanilla extract	5 mL
½ c.	milk	125 mL
⅓ c.	flour (sifted)	90 mL
1 t.	granulated sugar replacement	5 mL
3	egg whites (beaten stiff)	3

Beat egg yolks and bananas until well blended. Add vanilla, milk, flour and sugar replacement, beating to blend thoroughly. Gently and completely fold egg yolk mixture into stiffly beaten egg whites. Pour mixture into well-greased 1-qt. (1-L) baking dish, set dish in pan and add ½ in. (15 mm) water to pan. Bake at 325 °F (165 °C) for 30 minutes, or until lightly browned and puffy.

Microwave: Cook on Defrost for 15 to 17 minutes. Turn dish every 5 minutes.

Yield: 6 servings
Exchange 1 serving: 1 bread, ½ medium-fat meat
Calories 1 serving: 105

Daisy Cake

9	eggs (separated)	9
2 T.	liquid fructose	30 mL
1½ c.	flour (sifted)	375 mL
¾ t.	cream of tartar	4 mL
½ t.	baking powder	2 mL
½ t.	salt	2 mL
2 t.	lemon extract	10 mL

Beat egg whites and fructose until stiff. Beat egg yolks until fluffy and light yellow in color. Combine flour, cream of tartar, baking powder and salt in sifter. Add alternately with egg yolks to stiffened egg whites, beating continually, and add lemon extract. Pour into 10-in. (25-cm) angel-food cake pan. Bake at 325 °F (165 °C) for 55 to 60 minutes, or until done.

Yield: 20 servings
Exchange 1 serving: ½ bread, ½ fat
Calories 1 serving: 72

Coconut Cakes

2⅔ c.	cake flour (sifted)	625 mL
¼ t.	salt	1 mL
2 t.	baking powder	10 mL
½ c.	solid shortening (soft)	125 mL
3 T.	granulated sugar replacement	45 mL
2	eggs	2
1 t.	vanilla extract	5 mL
1½ c.	unsweetened coconut (flaked)	375 mL

Sift cake flour, salt and baking powder together. Beat shortening and sugar replacement until creamy and then beat in eggs and vanilla. Add flour mixture and coconut, stirring until well blended. Drop by teaspoonfuls onto lightly greased cookie sheets; press slightly with bottom of floured glass or tumbler. Bake at 375 °F (190 °C) for 12 minutes, or until done.

Yield: 36 cookies
Exchange 1 cookie: ½ fruit
                       1 fat
Calories 1 cookie: 65

FROSTINGS, TOPPINGS AND GLAZES

Powdered Sugar Replacement

2 c.	nonfat dry milk powder	500 mL
2 c.	cornstarch	500 mL
1 c.	granulated sugar replacement	250 mL

Combine all ingredients in food processor or blender. Whip until well blended and powdered.

Yield: 4 c. (1000 mL)
Exchange ¼ c. (60 mL): 1 bread **or** ½ nonfat milk
                                              ½ bread
Calories ¼ c. (60 mL): 81

Decorative Frosting

¼ c.	solid shortening (soft)	60 mL
½ t.	white vanilla extract	2 mL
¾ c.	Powdered Sugar Replacement (above)	190 mL
1 T.	milk	15 mL

Cream together shortening and vanilla until light and fluffy. Stir in powdered sugar replacement and milk until mixture is well blended. If frosting is too stiff, add a few drops of milk. Tint as desired. Make flowers with a pastry tube on waxed paper. Allow to harden in freezer and then quickly transfer onto the cake.

Yield: ½ c. (125 mL)
Exchange full recipe: 3 bread
                                     10 fat
Calories full recipe: 638

Butter Frosting

2 c.	skim milk	500 mL
5 T.	flour	75 mL
⅓ c.	butter	90 mL
⅓ c.	granulated sugar replacement	90 mL
1 T.	vanilla extract	15 mL
1	egg white (beaten stiff)	1

Combine milk and flour in saucepan. Cook and stir over low heat until a thick sauce results. Cool completely. Combine butter, sugar replacement and vanilla in mixing bowl, beating until fluffy. Add sauce mixture and beat until consistency of whipped cream. Fold in stiffly beaten egg white.

Yield: Frosts sides and tops of 9-in. (23-cm) layers or 30 cupcakes
Exchange 1/16 **recipe:** ⅕ bread
⅗ fat
Calories 1/16 **recipe:** 55

Coconut Pecan Frosting

1 c.	evaporated skimmed milk	250 mL
⅓ c.	granulated sugar replacement	90 mL
1	egg	1
1 T.	flour	15 mL
2 T.	margarine	30 mL
2 t.	vanilla extract	10 mL
¾ c.	unsweetened coconut	190 mL
⅓ c.	pecans (chopped)	90 mL

Combine milk, sugar replacement, egg, flour and margarine in saucepan. Cook and stir on low heat until mixture thickens and then remove from heat. Stir in vanilla, coconut and pecans; let cool slightly. Spread over cake while warm.

Yield: Frosts two 9-in. (23-cm) layers or 13 × 9-in. (33 × 23-cm) cake
Exchange 1/18 **recipe:** 1/7 bread
1 fat
Calories 1/18 **recipe:** 54

Seven-Minute Frosting

2	egg whites	2
¼ t.	cream of tartar	1 mL
⅓ c.	granulated sugar replacement	90 mL
⅓ c.	water	90 mL
¼ t.	salt	1 mL
1 t.	vanilla extract	5 mL

Combine egg whites, cream of tartar, sugar replacement, water and salt in top of double boiler, and beat until frothy. Place over boiling water, and beat mixture constantly until it thickens and will hold peaks. Remove from boiling water and beat in vanilla. Continue beating until smooth and of spreading consistency.

Yield: Frosts sides and tops of two 9-in. (23-cm) layers or 30 cupcakes
Exchange 1 serving: Negligible
Calories 1 serving: Negligible

Variations

CHOCOLATE: Add ¼ c. (60 mL) cocoa to egg-white mixture before beating. Continue with directions.

Exchange 1 serving: Negligible
Calories 1 serving: Negligible

FRUIT-FLAVORED: Add 2 t. (10 mL) desired flavoring plus food color to egg-white mixture before beating. Continue with directions.

Exchange 1 serving: Negligible
Calories 1 serving: Negligible

Jelly Frosting

½ c.	Juice Jelly (p. 94)	125 mL
2	egg whites	2
2 t.	granulated sugar replacement	10 mL

Combine Juice Jelly, egg whites and sugar replacement in top of double boiler; place over boiling water. Beat constantly until mixture thickens and holds stiff peaks. Remove from boiling water; continue to beat until smooth and of spreading consistency.

Yield: Frosts sides and tops of two 9-in. (23-cm) layers or 30 cupcakes
Exchange 1 serving: Negligible
Calories 1 serving: 4

Strawberry Topping

2 c.	fresh or frozen strawberries (unsweetened)	500 mL
1½ t.	cornstarch	7 mL
¼ c.	cold water	60 mL
2 t.	granulated sugar replacement	10 mL

Place strawberries in top of double boiler; cook over boiling water until soft and juicy. Blend cornstarch and cold water and add to strawberries. Cook until clear and slightly thickened. Remove from heat and add sugar replacement; cool. Topping can also be made with blueberries or raspberries.

Yield: 1½ c. (375 mL)
Exchange ½ c. (125 mL): 1 fruit
Calories ½ c. (125 mL): 40

Chocolate Topping

3 c.	skim milk	750 mL
2 oz.	unsweetened chocolate	60 g
3 T.	cornstarch	45 mL
½ c.	granulated sugar replacement	125 mL
1 t.	salt	5 mL
2 T.	butter	30 mL
2 t.	vanilla extract	10 mL

Combine milk, chocolate, cornstarch, sugar replacement and salt in saucepan. Bring to a full boil, and boil for 2 to 3 minutes; remove from heat. Add butter and vanilla.

Yield: 3 c. (750 mL)
Exchange 2 T. (30 mL): ½ fat
Calories 2 T. (30 mL): 35

Crumb Topping

⅓ c.	flour	90 mL
1 T.	granulated sugar replacement	15 mL
1 T.	liquid shortening	15 mL
½ t.	cinnamon	2 mL
¼ t.	nutmeg	1 mL

Combine all ingredients in mixing bowl, blender or food processor. Work until crumbly.

Yield: ⅓ c. (90 mL)
Exchange full recipe: 2 bread
                         3 fat
Calories full recipe: 265

Sweet Whipped Topping

1 env.	lo-cal whipped topping mix	1 env.
½ c.	water (ice cold)	125 mL
2 T.	Powdered Sugar Replacement (p. 134)	30 mL

Whip together topping mix and water until soft peaks form. Gradually add sugar replacement; whip until stiff.

Yield: 2 c. (500 mL)
Exchange 1 T. (15 mL): Negligible
Calories 1 T. (15 mL): 9

Spiced Whipped Topping

1 env.	lo-cal whipped topping mix	1 env.
dash each	nutmeg, cinnamon, allspice	dash each
½ c.	water (ice cold)	125 mL
1 T.	Powdered Sugar Replacement (p. 134)	15 mL

Combine topping mix and spices in mixing bowl; add water. Beat mixture until soft peaks form. Gradually add sugar replacement; beat to stiff peaks.

Yield: 2 c. (500 mL)
Exchange 1 T. (15 mL): Negligible
Calories 1 T. (15 mL): 9

Chocolate Whipped Topping

1 env.	lo-cal whipped topping mix	1 env.
2 T.	cocoa	30 mL
dash	salt	dash
½ t.	vanilla extract	2 mL
½ c.	water (ice cold)	125 mL
2 T.	Powdered Sugar Replacement (p. 134)	30 mL

Combine topping mix, cocoa and salt in mixing bowl; stir to blend. Add vanilla and water, and beat until soft peaks form. Gradually, add sugar replacement, and beat until mixture is stiff.

Yield: 2 c. (500 mL)
Exchange 1 T. (15 mL): Negligible
Calories 1 T. (15 mL): 11

Fruit-Flavored Whipped Topping

1 env.	lo-cal whipped topping mix	1 env.
1 env.	unsweetened fruit drink mix	1 env.
½ c.	water (ice cold)	125 mL
2 T.	Powdered Sugar Replacement (p. 134)	30 mL

Combine topping mix and soft drink mix in mixing bowl. Stir to blend; add water. Beat until soft peaks form. Gradually add sugar replacement; beat to stiff peaks.

Yield: 2 c. (500 mL)
Exchange 1 T. (15 mL): Negligible
Calories 1 T. (15 mL): 9

Coffee Whipped Topping

1 env.	lo-cal whipped topping mix	1 env.
½ c.	coffee (ice cold)	125 mL
1 T.	Powdered Sugar Replacement (p. 134)	15 mL

Whip together topping mix and coffee until soft peaks form. Gradually add sugar replacement; beat to stiff peaks.

Yield: 2 c. (500 mL)
Exchange 1 T. (15 mL): Negligible
Calories 1 T. (15 mL): 9

Vanilla Glaze

¼ c.	cold water	60 mL
2 t.	cornstarch	10 mL
dash	salt	dash
⅓ c.	granulated sugar replacement	90 mL
1 t.	vanilla extract	5 mL

Blend cold water and cornstarch and pour into small saucepan. Add salt. Boil until clear and thickened; remove from heat. Add sugar replacement and vanilla, stirring to dissolve, and cool.

Yield: ¼ c. (60 mL)
Exchange: Negligible
Calories: Negligible

Apple Glaze

1 c.	apple juice	250 mL
½ c.	water	125 mL
1 t.	cornstarch	5 mL
2 t.	liquid sugar replacement	10 mL
1 t.	margarine	5 mL

Combine juice, water and cornstarch in saucepan. Cook and stir until mixture is clear and slightly thickened; remove from heat. Add sugar replacement and margarine. Serve hot or cold.

Yield: 1¼ c. (310 mL)
Exchange ¼ c. (60 mL): ½ fruit
Calories ¼ c. (60 mL): 30

Dry Milk Glaze

½ c.	nonfat dry milk powder	125 mL
2 t.	granulated sugar replacement	10 mL
1 t.	vanilla extract	5 mL
1 T.	cold water	15 mL

Combine dry milk and sugar replacement in food processor or blender. Blend to fine powder, pour into small bowl, and add vanilla and water. Stir with fork until well blended. If glaze hardens too quickly, add a few drops of cold water. Stir to blend.

Yield: ½ c. (125 mL)
Exchange full recipe: 1½ bread
Calories full recipe: 120

Chocolate Drizzle

2 t.	cornstarch	10 mL
¼ c.	cold water	60 mL
dash	salt	dash
1 oz.	unsweetened chocolate	30 g
⅓ c.	granulated sugar replacement	90 mL
½ t.	butter	3 mL

Blend cornstarch and cold water and pour into small saucepan. Add salt and chocolate. Cook on low heat until chocolate melts and mixture is thick; remove from heat. Stir in sugar replacement and blend in butter. Use over cake or ice cream.

Yield: ⅓ c. (90 mL)
Exchange: Negligible
Calories: Negligible

NUTRITIONAL
INFORMATION OF
PREPARED PRODUCTS

Food manufacturers now label their products with nutritional information. This information can be very useful to anyone using the American Diabetes Association's exchange list in their diets. The labels give the number of calories and the grams of protein, carbohydrates and fat in each serving. Most often they are listed as in the example below.

NUTRITIONAL INFORMATION PER SERVING
Servings per container: 12
Serving Size (Cookie): 3
Calories per serving: 170
Protein: 2 g
Carbohydrates: 22 g
Fat: 7 g

With this information you can work out the food exchange on any product. The exchange list below is needed for calculations.

Exchange	Calories	Carbohydrate (grams)	Protein (grams)	Fat (grams)
Milk				
Whole	170	12	8	10
2%	125	12	8	5
Skim	80	12	8	0
Vegetable	36	7	2	0
Fruit	40	10	0	0
Bread	68	15	2	0
Meat				
Lean	55	0	7	3
Medium Fat	78	0	7	6
High Fat	100	0	7	8
Fat	45	0	0	5

Compare the nutrient value on the label with the nutrient values on the exchange list. Count whole and nearest half exchanges.

	Exchange	C	P	F
1. List the grams of carbohydrates, protein and fat per serving.		22	2	7
2. Subtract carbohydrates first. Bread exchange has 15 carbohydrates + 2 protein.	1 bread	−15	−2	
		7	0	7
3. Compare the next nearest carbohydrate exchange. Fruit exchange has 10.	1 fruit	−10		
		0	0	7
4. Compare fat exchange.	1 fat			−5
		0	0	2

You have 2 grams of fat left—or approximately ½ fat exchange; therefore, your exchange on 1 serving of this product is equivalent to 1 bread, 1 fruit, 1½ fat.

5. Check with calories.
   1 bread =   68 calories
   1 fruit   =   40 calories
   1½ fat   =   67 calories
            175   (Product information states 170.)

Most exchanges figured on foods are not exact.

SELECTED PREPARED PRODUCTS

BORDENS FOODS*

Product	Serving Size	Calories	Protein (grams)	Carbohydrates (grams)	Fat (grams)
Snacks					
Wise—Corn chips	1 oz.	160	2	16	10
Wise—Potato chips	1 oz.	150	2	14	10
Wise—Popcorn (Butter-flavored)	1 c.	70	1	8	4

For more information about Bordens products, write Corporate Nutrition, Borden, Inc., 990 Kingsmill Parkway, Columbus, OH 43229.

DANNON

Product	Serving Size	Calories	Protein (grams)	Carbohydrates (grams)	Fat (grams)
Yogurt					
Plain	8 oz.	150	12	17	4
Flavored	8 oz.	200	11	32	4
Fruit	8 oz.	260	10	49	3

* Products in the following charts use fructose, aspartame, sorbitol or a product thereof as sugar replacements. They contain no sugar.

DIA-MEL BRAND

Product	Serving Size	Exchange
Preserves and jellies		
All varieties	1 t.	Free
Gels		
All flavors of mixes	½ c.	¼ fruit
Ready to eat varieties	4 oz.	Free
Puddings		
All flavors	½ c.	½ nonfat milk ½ fruit
Cake mixes		
All mixes	⅒ cake	1 bread ½ fat
Cookie mixes		
Oatmeal, chocolate chip cookies	2	½ bread ½ fat
Pancake mix	3 cakes	1½ bread
Sweeteners & syrups		
Table syrup	1 T.	Free
Chocolate syrup	2 T.	¼ fruit
Sweet'n-it	5 drops	Free
Sugarlike	1 pkt.	Free

For more information on Dia-Mel Brand products, write The Estee Corp., Professional Services Division, 169 Lackawanna Avenue, Parsippany, NJ 07054.

ESTEE CORP. *

Product	Serving Size	Calories	Protein (grams)	Carbohydrates (grams)	Fat (grams)	Exchange
FRUCTOSE SWEETENED:						
Cake Mix						
White	1/10th cake	76	1	18	1	1 bread 1 fruit
Lemon	1/10th cake	81	1	19	1	1 bread 1 fruit
Chocolate	1/10th cake	88	2	21	1	1 bread 1 fruit
Cookies						For 2 cookies:
Vanilla, Lemon	1	24	trace	3	1	½ bread ½ fat
Oatmeal Raisin	1	23	trace	3	1	½ bread ½ fat
Coconut	1	25	trace	3	2	½ bread ½ fat
Chocolate Chip	1	27	trace	3	1	½ bread ½ fat
Fudge	1	25	trace	3	1	½ bread ½ fat

For more information about Estee's foods, write The Estee Corporation, Professional Services Division, 169 Lackawanna Ave., Parsippany, NJ 07054.
* Prepared as directed on package.

Product	Serving Size	Calories	Protein (grams)	Carbohydrates (grams)	Fat (grams)	Exchange
Fructose						
Granulated	1 t.	15	0	4	0	⅓ fruit
Liquid	½ t.	10	0	3	0	¼ fruit
Gels						
Dry Mix and Ready to Eat	½ c.	40	0	10	0	1 fruit
Pudding						
Chocolate	½ c.	90	5	17	trace	½ c. = ½ nonfat milk 1 fruit
Vanilla	½ c.	85	6	15	trace	½ c. = ½ nonfat milk 1 fruit
Lemon	½ c.	104	trace	26	trace	½ c. = 1 bread 1 fruit
SORBITOL SWEETENED:						
Boxed Chocolates						
Coated raisin candies	6	33	1	4	2	10 candies = ½ bread ½ fat
Estee-ets with peanut candies	5	35	1	4	2	8 candies = ½ bread ½ fat

Estee cont.

Product	Serving Size	Calories	Protein (grams)	Carbohydrates (grams)	Fat (grams)	Exchange
TV mix candies	4	35	1	3	2	10 candies = ½ bread 1 fat
Peanut butter cup candies	1	44	1	3	3	2 candies = ½ bread 1 fat
Chocolate Bars						
Almond sections	3	100	2	8	8	½ bread ½ fat
Fruit and nut sections	3	98	1	8	7	½ bread ½ fat
Milk chocolate sections	3	100	1	8	8	½ bread 1½ fat
Bittersweet sections	3	102	1	8	8	½ bread 1½ fat
Crunch sections	3	78	1	7	6	½ bread 1 fat
Toasted bran sections	3	97	1	9	7	½ bread 1½ fat

Product	Serving Size	Calories	Protein (grams)	Carbohydrates (grams)	Fat (grams)	Exchange
Coconut sections	3	104	1	8	8	½ bread 1½ fat
Cookies Lemon & Duplex	1	50	1	8	3	½ bread ½ fat
Gum Drops Fruit, licorice	4	11	0	3	trace	7 candies: ½ fruit
Crème-filled wafers Chocolate	1	23	trace	3	1	2 wafers: ½ bread ½ fat
Vanilla	1	24	trace	3	1	
Assorted	1	35	1	4	2	3 wafers: 1 bread ½ fat
Hard candy Assorted Peppermint Tropi-Mix	2	23	0	6	0	½ fruit
Rolled mints All flavors	1	4	0	1	trace	5 mints: ½ fruit

FEATHERWEIGHT

Product	Serving Size	Calories	Protein (grams)	Carbohy-drates (grams)	Fat (grams)
FRUIT IN JUICE—RED LABEL					
Apricots	½c.	50	1	12	0
Grapefruit Segments	½ c.	40	0	9	0
Fruit Cocktail	½ c.	50	1	12	0
Peaches	½ c.	50	1	13	0
Pears	½ c.	60	0	15	0
Pineapple	½ c.	70	0	18	0
FRUIT IN WATER—BLUE LABEL					
Applesauce	½ c.	50	0	13	0
Light Grapes	½ c.	60	1	13	0
Mandarin Oranges	½ c.	35	0	8	0
Apricots	½ c.	35	0	9	0
Dark Cherries	½ c.	60	1	13	0
Light Cherries	½ c.	50	1	11	0
Fruit Cocktail	½ c.	40	0	10	0
Peaches	½ c.	30	0	8	0
Pineapple	½ c.	60	0	15	0
Purple Plums	½ c.	40	1	9	0

DESSERTS (artificially sweetened and without added salt):

Product	Serving Size	Calories	Protein (grams)	Carbohy-drates (grams)	Fat (grams)
Pudding					
Butterscotch	½ c.	50	4	9	0
Chocolate	½ c.	60	5	9	0
Vanilla	½ c.	50	4	9	0
Gelatin					
Strawberry	½ c.	10	2	0	0
Cherry	½ c.	10	2	0	0
Lemon	½ c.	10	2	0	0
Lime	½ c.	10	2	0	0
Orange	½ c.	10	2	0	0
Jellies (with a small amount of fructose syrup)					
All flavors	1 T.	16	0	4	0

Product	Serving Size	Calories	Protein (grams)	Carbohy-drates (grams)	Fat (grams)
Preserves and marmalade (with a small amount of fructose syrup)					
All flavors	1 T.	16	0	4	0
Syrups (with a small amount of fructose syrup)					
Blueberry	1 T.	14	0	3	0
Pancake	1 T.	12	0	3	0
Chocolate Fla-vored	1 T.	30	0	7	0
Jellies, preserves (artificially sweetened with saccharin)					
All flavors	1 T.	6	0	1	0
SWEETS (not calorie controlled):					
Candies					
Assorted Hard Candy	1	12	0	3	0
Gum and breath mints					
Gum, all flavors	1 pc.	4	0	1	0
Mints, all flavors	1 pc.	4	0	1	0.5
Cookies					
Chocolate Chip, Lemon, Vanilla, Chocolate Crescent	1	40	1	4	2
Chocolate Crème, Vanilla Crème, Peanut Butter Crème Wafers	1	40	0	4	2
Sandwich Crème	1	50	1	6	2
Chocolate-Flavored Bar	2	90	2	8	6
Rice Crisp Bar	2	100	2	9	6

For more information about FEATHERWEIGHT products, write to Chicago Dietetic Supply, Inc., PO Box 40, La Grange, IL 60525.

GENERAL FOODS*

Product	Serving Size	Calories	Protein (grams)	Carbohydrates (grams)	Fat (grams)
Gelatin					
D-Zerta Low Calorie Gelatin All flavors	½	8	2	0	0
D-Zerta Low Calorie Pudding and Pie Filling (prepared with nonfat milk)					
Butterscotch	½ c.	70	4	12	0
Chocolate	½ c.	70	5	12	0
Vanilla	½ c.	70	4	13	0
D-Zerta Low Calorie Whipped Topping Mix	1 T.	8	0	0	1

* Prepared as directed on package

PILLSBURY

Product	Serving Size	Calories	Protein (grams)	Carbohydrates (grams)	Fat (grams)
Sweeteners					
Sweet 10	⅛ t.	0	0	0	0
Sprinkle Sweet	⅛ t.	2	0	0.5	0

The serving sizes of foods on the WEIGHT WATCHERS Program are not identical to the serving sizes of exchanges on the Diabetic Diet. It is quite possible to convert WEIGHT WATCHERS Program equivalencies to diabetic exchanges. This should be done, however, on the advice of your physician.

Weight Watchers International

Note that the column headings listed correspond to the following headings indicated in previous charts:

Product	Serving Size	Calories	Protein (grams)	Carbohy- drates (grams)	Fat (grams)	Exchange

	Portion Size	Calories	Protein (gm)	Carbohy-drates (gm)	Fat (gm)	WEIGHT WATCHERS program equivalencies
Apple Snacks	½ oz.	50	1	13	1	1 fruit
Fruit snacks						
Cinnamon	½ oz.	50	1	13	1	1 fruit
Peach	½ oz.	50	1	13	1	1 fruit
Strawberry	½ oz.	50	1	13	1	1 fruit
Sweet'ner—Granulated						
Sugar Substitute	1 indiv. packet	3.5	0	1	0	Use in reasonable amounts.
Soft drinks						
Black Cherry	12 fl. oz.	2	0	<1	0	2 cal. Specialty Foods
Cherry Cola	12 fl. oz.	2	0	<1	0	2 cal. Specialty Foods
Chocolate	12 fl. oz.	2	0	<1	0	2 cal. Specialty Foods
Cola	12 fl. oz.	0	0	<1	0	0 cal. Specialty Foods
Crème	12 fl. oz.	2	0	<1	0	2 cal. Specialty Foods
Frosta	12 fl. oz.	4	0	1	0	4 cal. Specialty Foods
Ginger Ale	12 fl. oz.	2	0	<1	0	2 cal. Specialty Foods
Grape	12 fl. oz.	0	0	<1	0	0 cal. Specialty Foods

WEIGHT WATCHERS INTERNATIONAL—UNITED STATES *continued*

	Portion Size	Calories	Protein (gm)	Carbohydrates (gm)	Fat (gm)	WEIGHT WATCHERS program equivalencies
Lemon-Lime	12 fl. oz.	4	0	1	0	4 cal. Specialty Foods
Orange	12 fl. oz.	2	0	<1	0	2 cal. Specialty Foods
Raspberry	12 fl. oz.	2	0	<1	0	2 cal. Specialty Foods
Rootbeer	12 fl. oz.	0	0	<1	0	0 cal. Specialty Foods
Strawberry	12 fl. oz.	2	0	<1	0	2 cal. Specialty Foods

WEIGHT WATCHERS INTERNATIONAL FOOD PRODUCT INFORMATION—CANADA

	Portion Size	Calories	Protein (gm)	Carbohydrates (gm)	Fat (gm)	WEIGHT WATCHERS program equivalencies
Calorie & carbohydrate reduced fruits						
Unpeeled Apricot Halves	4 halves with 2 T. juice	42.9	0	10.5	0	1 fruit
Fruit cocktail	½ c.	42.9	0	11.9	0	1 fruit

155

WEIGHT WATCHERS INTERNATIONAL—CANADA continued

	Portion Size	Calories	Protein (gm)	Carbohydrates (gm)	Fat (gm)	WEIGHT WATCHERS program equivalencies
Peach halves	2 halves with 2 T. juice	41.5	0	11.5	0	1 fruit
Sliced peaches	½ c.	42.9	0	11.9	0	1 fruit
Pear halves	2 halves with 2 T. juice	44.1	0	12.3	0	1 fruit
Plain yogurt	½ c.	46	5	6.3	0.2	1 milk
Calorie reduced fruit yogurts						
Blueberry	1 container (175 gm)	88.2	6.5	15.4	0.6	¾ milk, ½ fruit
Raspberry	1 container (175 gm)	90.8	6.6	15.9	0.4	¾ milk, ½ fruit
Strawberry	1 container (175 gm)	90.3	6.5	15	.04	¾ milk, ½ fruit
Calorie reduced fudge bar	1 bar (75 mL)	42.8	2.4	7.6	.29	¼ milk, ½ fruit

WEIGHT WATCHERS INTERNATIONAL—CANADA continued

	Portion Size	Calories	Protein (gm)	Carbohydrates (gm)	Fat (gm)	WEIGHT WATCHERS program equivalencies
Calorie reduced gelatin desserts						
Cherry	½ cup	19	2	3	0	19 Cal. Specialty Foods
Lime	½ cup	19	2	3	0	19 Cal. Specialty Foods
Raspberry	½ cup	19	2	3	0	19 Cal. Specialty Foods
Strawberry	½ cup	19	2	3	0	19 Cal. Specialty Foods
Calorie reduced iced tea mix	8 fl. oz.	20	0	5	0	20 Cal. Specialty Foods
Low calorie sodas						
Cola	1 fl. oz.	.09	0	.008	0	.09 Cal. Specialty Foods
Ginger Ale	1 fl. oz.	.1	0	.02	0	.1 Cal. Specialty Foods
Lemon–Lime	1 fl. oz.	.2	0	.04	0	.2 Cal. Specialty Foods
Orange	1 fl. oz.	.2	0	.02	0	.2 Cal. Specialty Foods
Root-Beer	1 fl. oz.	.2	0	.03	0	.2 Cal. Specialty Foods
Low calorie sweetener	1 sachet	3	0	1	0	Use in reasonable amounts.

Index

159